The Art and Science
of Smalltalk

Hewlett-Packard Professional Books

The Art and Science of Smalltalk

Simon Lewis
Hewlett-Packard

Prentice Hall

London New York Toronto Sydney Tokyo Singapore Madrid Mexico City Munich

First published 1995 by
Prentice Hall International (UK) Limited
Campus 400, Maylands Avenue
Hemel Hempstead
Hertfordshire, HP2 7EZ
A division of
Simon & Schuster International Group

Printed and bound in Great Britain by
TJ Press Limited, Padstow, Cornwall

Library of Congress Cataloging-in-Publication Data

Lewis, Simon.
     The art and science of smalltalk/Simon Lewis.
         p.   cm. – (Hewlett-Packard professional books)
     Includes index.
     ISBN 0-13-371345-8
     1. Smalltalk (Computer program language)   I. Title.   II. Series.
     QA76.73.S59L48   1995   94-45966
     005.13'3–dc20   CIP

British Library Cataloguing in Publication Data

A catalogue record for this book is available
from the British Library

ISBN 0-13-371345-8

3 4 5   99 98 97 96 95

Contents

Part II The Art of Smalltalk

Preface

This book has been written to help you to help yourself. You may be considering adopting Smalltalk for your next project. You may have just started to program in Smalltalk. You may have been doing it for a while. Whatever your level of experience you'll know that Smalltalk is different. It's different from C, different even from C++, different to almost anything you'll have used before. These differences help give Smalltalk the power and productivity for which it is famous, but it's only by knowing how to exploit the differences that you can harness this power for yourself.

Smalltalk is different from other languages not only in its syntax (the parts of the language and how they go together), but in its whole philosophy of programming. Few programming languages are as interactive as Smalltalk. Fewer still make nearly all their source-code visible to the programmer on-line. This combination of features makes Smalltalk very powerful, but it can also make it intimidating to learn. This book aims to de-mystify that process by providing a practical rather than an academic introduction.

The huge code library that comes with Smalltalk is also a key part of its power. But which classes do what, which should you reuse, and which should you subclass? The aim of this book is to teach you the things you *need* to know to be able to program effectively in Smalltalk. You'll also learn which parts of the system you can safely ignore. You'll learn how to design your own classes, and how to use the existing ones. You'll learn how and when to use inheritance. You'll learn how to make the best use of the development tools, and how to split the work among the members of a team. Most of all, you'll learn how to adopt the Smalltalk *style*—how to find out what you need to know, without going to the manual. *The Art and Science of Smalltalk* is not just for programmers though. Managers or leaders of teams using Smalltalk should find a lot to interest them, especially in Part II.

This book is not an introduction to programming. It is assumed that you have at least some experience of another language. Experience in C, BASIC, Pascal, COBOL, or any similar language is fine. Familiarity with using (though not necessarily programming with), a graphical user-interface is also essential. Microsoft Windows, the Macintosh UI, or the X window system are good examples.

The Art and Science of Smalltalk is not a methodology. It's not intended to give you a defined process that you can feed your problem into at one end, and have Smalltalk code come out of at the other. Sometimes, competing views of how things should be done will be presented. You'll have to decide which philosophy to adopt in your particular circumstances, but you will be making an *informed* decision. In this way, the book is not prescriptive, but instead it's 'assistive'. It's also not a tutorial. You are however invited—in fact you're encouraged—to try things out using the system. Smalltalk style supports this, and you should experiment whenever something is not clear, or you want to confirm or enhance your understanding.

You should treat this book as complementary to the documentation that comes with Smalltalk. The manual tells you how to install and fire-up Smalltalk, and gives detailed and up-to-date descriptions of all the tools and many of the key system classes. Although this book includes an introduction to object-oriented programming (OOP), Smalltalk, and the development environment, its main purpose is to tell you how to make *use* of the tools, and how to use and reuse the system classes to maximum effect. It tells you the things you would otherwise only learn through experience.

The knowledge contained in the book has been gained from the practical experiences of the author and several of his colleagues over many years of Smalltalk programming. It applies specifically to the version of Smalltalk marketed by ParcPlace Digitalk as *VisualWorks* (and its predecessor—*ObjectWorks\Smalltalk*). However, because much of the discussion concerns the most basic principles and classes, it should be broadly applicable to other Smalltalks.

Knowledge about Smalltalk can be divided into three kinds. First, there is basic knowledge about the language, its fundamental concepts, and core classes. Second, there is knowledge about the Smalltalk 'style', or philosophy of programming. Third, there is detailed knowledge about the specifics of the rest of the class hierarchy. This book is divided into two parts. The first part, *The Science of Smalltalk*, provides an introduction to OOP, and an introduction to the most important tools and classes in the Smalltalk system. It'll help you with the first kind of knowledge. The second part of the book, *The Art of Smalltalk*, concentrates on how to use those classes and tools in the very best way. It'll help you with the second kind of knowledge. Together, these two kinds of knowledge will help you gain for yourself the third kind of knowledge—an understanding of the detailed (and frequently changeable) facilities of the complete code library.

The Smalltalk system is large and complex and it does take time to learn and be comfortable with. However, if you follow the simple advice given in this book you'll soon be enjoying the benefits of Smalltalk. You'll be getting better code reuse by properly understanding the system classes. You'll be writing programs which are easier to understand and easier to maintain because they go with the flow of the system, not against it. You'll know how best to organise small teams of people working together in Smalltalk. Most of all, you'll know what to do when you don't understand something. You'll be able to help yourself.

Typographic Conventions

Like most computer books, this book uses a couple of typeface conventions to distinguish literal computer expressions from the main text. Wherever Smalltalk classes, methods or expressions are written they are shown like this: `MyObject display`. In contrast, whenever a command from a pop-up menu or button is being referred to, it is shown like this: **implementors**.

Acknowledgements

Lots of the basic ideas in this book came from discussions with friends and colleagues at HP Labs in Bristol. Many other people carefully read and commented on various parts of the manuscript whilst it was in preparation, and others simply provided much needed help and encouragement along the way. The folks involved included Richard Brown, Janet Bruten, Dave Clarke, Enrico Coiera, Richard Dykema, Jonathan Griffin, Leo Grondin, Caroline Knight, Wendy Odlum, Siani Pearson, Jo Reid, Brenda Romans, Steven Scott, David Stephenson, Kristen Stevenson, Viki Williams and others who I'm sure I've forgotten to mention. To all these people I would like to offer my sincere thanks.

The Science of Smalltalk

Some Advice on Getting Started

If you're absolutely new to Smalltalk this chapter is for you. You're about to undertake a task (learning Smalltalk) which can be both very rewarding and yet at the same time very uncomfortable. One of the aims of this book is to make that task more rewarding and less uncomfortable. The aim of this first chapter is to help you start off in the right way. We'll be looking briefly at how to manage the transition to object-oriented programming (OOP) and Smalltalk, mention a few things to look out for, and set the scene for the rest of the book. The actual management of Smalltalk projects is something we'll return to in some more detail in the very last chapter.

The things you might consider doing to smooth your path towards Smalltalk proficiency will differ depending on your circumstances, background, experience, goals, resources and so on. Consequently this chapter presents a range of different suggestions and ideas which are known to have worked for other people in a similar position to your own in the past.

If you're already using Smalltalk, you should still find some things of interest here. In fact if you're currently having any particular difficulty, you may even discover where you are going wrong. However, if you think that this chapter might not be for you, then feel free to skip to the later chapters.

The Smalltalk Learning Curve

Learning a new language is never completely painless. Sadly, with Smalltalk you have to learn a little bit more than just a new language. You may have to learn about object-oriented programming, learn the

Smalltalk language itself, learn how to use the *VisualWorks* development environment, learn how to write your own Smalltalk code and learn how to reuse the code in the system's code-library. Most significantly, you'll probably have to learn a whole new way of going about solving your programming problems.

Many newcomers to Smalltalk find that although they start off very enthusiastically, their enthusiasm falls off rapidly as their level of discomfort with all the changes they must absorb rises. This is entirely natural because programming in Smalltalk is so different from programming in many other languages. The extent of these differences gives rise to a characteristic Smalltalk 'learning curve' shown qualitatively in the diagram below. The steepness and length of this curve will of course depend on your previous experience, and to a large extent on your expectations. Broadly speaking though, you should expect it to take anything from two weeks to six months before you stop feeling *less* comfortable every day and start feeling *more* comfortable all the time with programming in Smalltalk.

Luckily there are some positive steps that you can take to both reduce the peak level of discomfort and shorten the amount of time it takes to get over the peak of the learning curve.

Be Prepared for a Culture Shock

It can't be stressed enough that Smalltalk is different from other programming languages. It's not just that you might be doing OOP for

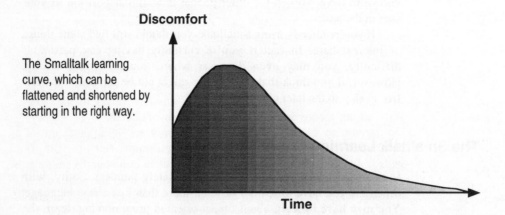

The Smalltalk learning curve, which can be flattened and shortened by starting in the right way.

Discomfort

Time

the very first time (as if that wasn't enough!). There are real management and technical differences between Smalltalk and other languages. For example, Smalltalk promotes and safely supports a much more interactive and exploratory programming style than other languages. That's where it gets its legendary productivity. Now this does *not* mean that Smalltalk programs don't have to be *designed*. What it does mean is that if you want to get the most out of Smalltalk, you have to adopt a more iterative design and programming style than you may be used to. This can be very uncomfortable, especially if you are used to developing systems using a traditional 'single-pass' or 'waterfall' methodology.

On the technical side, being a complete programming language, Smalltalk can do all the things other languages can do. Very often though you will find that it does them in completely different ways. For example, if you are used to writing applications with graphical user-interfaces (GUIs) on PCs, Macintoshes or Unix workstations, you will find that Smalltalk GUIs can do all the same things. However, they are built in a completely different way (mainly because for historical reasons the Smalltalk user-interface works by 'polling', rather than by being event-driven).

These kinds of differences can make you feel like giving up because much of your hard-won knowledge and experience *seems* to be of less use in a Smalltalk environment. It's another aim of this book to show you that that isn't necessarily the case.

Start Off Small

It may seem obvious but it's still worth saying—choose something small for your first Smalltalk exercise. Trying to build something even a fraction of the size of the systems you're used to building first time around is asking for trouble. Starting small will greatly help to reduce the culture shock we talked about above. It also goes without saying that you should probably try Smalltalk out on an experimental project first, rather than launching straight into a 'mission critical' application. What all this means depends on your situation of course.

If you're a manager planning to migrate a large team of programmers over to Smalltalk, then it is significantly better to start off with just two or three people. Try to give them complete freedom to explore the new technology and get themselves over the peak of the learning curve. They will then become the local experts who'll be able to help the rest of the team climb the curve.

If you're a member of such a team, or you're learning Smalltalk as an individual, there are a number of things you can do yourself. If you're lucky enough to have access to someone else's Smalltalk programs try modifying them in simple ways. If not, try working on a subset of your programming problem. For example, try representing some of the key data structures as Smalltalk objects, or try building a key window dialogue using the *VisualWorks* GUI development tools.

Explore and Work Interactively

One of the things that makes Smalltalk so powerful is its interactive programming environment. The more use you can make of this environment, the quicker you will get up the learning curve and the smaller the culture shock will be. Remember that you can create and execute snippets of code in seconds. This is ideal when you don't quite understand how a particular feature works. Don't spend ages looking through the manual trying to understand it. Sadly, you can't learn Smalltalk from a book. Experiment! Experienced Smalltalk programmers use the manual less than beginners, not because they know more about the system, but because they've learned how to use the system to *find out* what they need to know. This is a skill we'll be talking about a lot in Part II — *The Art of Smalltalk*.

Even if it takes half an hour or more to set up an experiment to test how something works, it is frequently well worth doing it because you will get a definitive answer. It really is worth experimenting. All this experimentation brings its own caveat though:

Be Prepared to Throw Code Away

It is very easy to build up a lot of code in Smalltalk—it's a very productive environment after all. However, when you've finished experimenting you've got to be prepared to throw your code away. This doesn't mean you should go through a strict experimental phase and then rewrite everything from scratch though. What it means is that you should take advantage of the fact that your second attempt at programming something will be immeasurably better than the first. This may well be true in many languages, but in most you couldn't *afford* to take advantage of it. In Smalltalk not only will your second attempt be better, it'll take you a fraction of the time to produce. It's well worth doing it.

Get Some Help

This may seem obvious, but if you can enlist the help of someone who has a reasonable amount of Smalltalk experience, the whole process of climbing the learning curve and becoming self sufficient will be made very much easier. Not only will you avoid spending hours trying to find the answer to a simple question, you will also find it much easier to start programming in a good Smalltalk 'style' straight away. Again, another of the aims of this book is to help you adopt a good Smalltalk style from the start.

You might be able to find someone to help you from within your organisation, or you may have to look outside. Remember though that Smalltalk is different even from other interactive object-oriented languages. Make sure you work with someone with specific *Smalltalk* experience.

Of course if you can't get help, or even if you can, reading this book is also a very good way to help yourself up the learning curve. However, if you're going to help yourself, the *very* best way is to make sure you've got the Smalltalk system up and running. Exploring and trying things out is really the only way to test your understanding of the concepts of object-oriented programming and Smalltalk that we'll be discussing from now on.

Where To From Here?

The Art and Science of Smalltalk is intended to help you to learn about and understand the Smalltalk language, code-library and development system which underlies the *VisualWorks* programming environment (and some others). The book itself is divided into two parts.

Part I — *The Science of Smalltalk*, provides an introduction to Smalltalk itself. We'll look at the basic concepts of OOP, talk about the Smalltalk language, and cover some of the most important classes in the system library. We'll also look briefly at the development environment, but you should be prepared to take some responsibility for getting yourself up and running in this area. The idea is to provide you with the basic knowledge you'll need to find out for yourself about those parts of the system you really need to understand. That's why we don't cover the whole system in exhaustive depth.

The second part of the book, *The Art of Smalltalk*, covers some of the more difficult, non-specific issues involved in working with Smalltalk. We'll look at how to design Smalltalk programs (how, if you like, to *do* object-oriented programming). We'll also consider how to code in Smalltalk, and how to make full use of the facilities of the development environment (including a whole chapter on debugging). Finally, we'll look in some more detail at how to manage Smalltalk projects.

All that's to come. The very next chapter, *An Introduction to Objects*, starts right at the beginning. If you've never done any OOP before, this is the place to start. If however, you're confident you know what OOP is all about (and don't feel in need of a refresher course) but have never done any Smalltalk, start with Chapter 3—*An Introduction to Smalltalk*. Good luck and remember, Smalltalk is supposed to be fun.

An Introduction to Objects

Smalltalk is an *object-oriented* programming language. Object-oriented programming consists of designing and implementing objects, and specifying their interactions. Whether you do this directly or through a development environment like *VisualWorks* does not matter. What you are doing is creating objects. But what is an object? That is the question this chapter sets out to answer. Later on we'll look at how to use objects to write programs, but for now we'll just consider what we might call 'object anatomy'.

The description *object-oriented* applies to lots of different languages. It encompasses a set of concepts which are broadly similar in all those languages. These concepts include the notions of class and instance, and concepts such as messaging, encapsulation, instantiation, inheritance, and polymorphism. Although these are general concepts, we will discuss them here in the specific form in which they apply to Smalltalk. Remember that some other object-oriented languages may not have all these concepts, and others may introduce additional ones. Even languages which share the same concepts may implement them in different ways. Be wary of this if you have had exposure to OOP through other languages.

In spite of any differences, if you *have* previously programmed in another object-oriented language you should find the contents of this chapter very familiar. On the other hand, if you haven't done any OOP before you may find some of the concepts presented here a little strange. Don't despair—it'll start to make sense as you go through the rest of book, and as you start to program in Smalltalk and really understand how objects behave.

What is an Object?

Objects are discrete, self-contained, combinations of code and data. The diagram below shows one way to imagine what an object is like. In Smalltalk, the code in an object is split into pieces called *methods*, and the data is held in *variables* of various types. A program might contain thousands of these objects, which can vary in size from only a few bytes to many kilobytes. Objects can represent things in the real world (like cheques, people or the week's shopping), or things in the computer world (like arrays, windows or event queues).

The diagram below deliberately shows the code as if it is surrounding the data. This is because the variables in each object can be accessed only by the methods in that particular object, and not by any other code. This is an example of the concept known in OOP as *encapsulation*.

Methods are somewhat similar to subroutines, functions, or procedures in other languages. They are self-contained snippets of code which have a name, can be individually called or invoked, and return a value when they have finished running. Smalltalk methods are invoked by sending a *message* to the relevant object. The message will contain the name of the method, as well as any necessary parameters. If the object being sent the message contains the method named in the message it is said to *understand* the message, and will execute the method, returning the result. As the diagram on the next page shows, the object which sends the message is called the *sender*, and the object which executes the message is called the *receiver*.

It might seem as if this sort of interaction between objects implies a sort of parallel processing, with objects sending messages to each other in parallel. In fact, the sender of a message is blocked until the

An object consists of some program code and some data, tightly bound together.

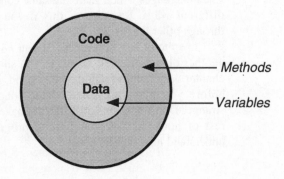

10

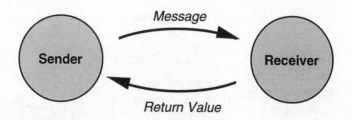

An object's methods are invoked by other objects sending messages to it.

message returns. In order to run the method, the receiver may send further messages, and is itself then blocked until those messages return. In this respect, sending a message is just like calling a function in a non-object-oriented language—there is no implication of parallel processing (although separately, Smalltalk does support its own light-weight 'threads' or processes).

The variables inside an object are similar to variables in non-OO languages. They each have a name and contain a value. However, as we shall discuss later, and unlike many other languages, Smalltalk variables do not have a type (such as integer or string). All variables are capable of holding any type of object.

Defining and Creating Objects

As we have observed, programming in an object-oriented language like Smalltalk consists of designing objects and specifying their interactions. This means deciding what data each object will hold in its variables, and writing the methods that will act upon that data. But objects are not designed individually. The programmer does not have to specify every object in the program personally. This would be very wasteful, because so many objects in a program are actually alike. Instead, the programmer specifies special objects, known in Smalltalk as *classes*. These classes act like templates or blueprints. Their task is to represent the functionality (the methods and the variables) that the programmer wants to put in the other objects in the program. These other objects are known in Smalltalk as *instances*. You can think of every object in Smalltalk as being *either* a class, *or* an instance.

As well as acting as templates, Smalltalk classes have another purpose. They are actually responsible for making the instance objects

11

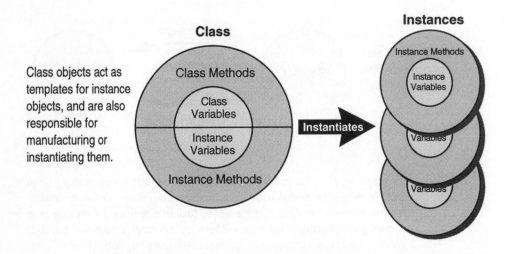

Class objects act as templates for instance objects, and are also responsible for manufacturing or instantiating them.

they represent. This process is called *instantiation,* as is shown in the diagram above. So, Smalltalk classes act both as templates for instances, and as factories which manufacture the instances they represent. Every instance is said to be an *instance of* the particular class which both manufactured it and represents it in template form.

This relationship between classes and instances means that class objects combine two types of code and data. There is the code and data which the class object *itself* contains (known as class methods and class variables), and there is the template for the code and data which *instances* of the class will contain (known as instance methods and instance variables). The class methods and variables implement the functionality which is associated with the actual manufacture of instances. The instance methods and variables do whatever the programmer has designed instances of this class to do.

Class objects only understand *class* methods, and instance objects only understand *instance* methods. This is a very important distinction, which frequently causes confusion. It is as well to try to get it clear in your mind before starting to program. If you expect your objects (classes and instances) to understand the messages you send them, you must send classes class messages and instances instance messages!

Every instance of a particular class has its *own set* of the instance variables defined in that class. They are not shared amongst instances. So, if a class defines an instance variable called 'size', every instance of that class will have a separate variable called 'size'. The values of all these 'size' variables can, and probably will, be different. The situation is different for class variables. These are defined in the class, but are visible to and shared between all instances of that class.

Although conceptually we might think that every instance of a class has its own identical copy of the instance methods defined in that class, in practice this would be very inefficient. So in Smalltalk, instances share the methods defined in their class. This means that if you alter the definition of an instance method in a class, all existing and future instances of that class will see and use the new definition.

All this class and instance stuff is rather complicated, so here is a summary:

Instance Variables
> A separate set in every instance (not shared).

Class Variables
> One set shared between the class and all its instances.

Instance Methods
> Defined in the class, but only understood by instances.

Class Methods
> Defined in the class, and only understood by the class.

Inheritance

We now know that because lots of Smalltalk objects are similar to each other, programmers don't design each and every one individually. Instead, they create objects called classes, which are templates for objects called instances. You might think that a programmer could now go off and start writing classes, ask those classes to make instances of themselves, and thereby create a Smalltalk program. In theory this is true, but in practice not only are lots of instances similar to each other, but lots of classes are too. Smalltalk programmers take advantage of this similarity between classes using a concept called *inheritance*.

Inheritance allows the programmer to say in effect *'This new class is just like that existing one, except in the following ways.'* The new class is called a *subclass*, and the existing class is called a *superclass*. When two classes are related in this way the subclass is said to *inherit from* the superclass. In Smalltalk, classes can have many subclasses which inherit from them. However, each subclass can only inherit directly from one superclass. Every class can be *both* a subclass *and* a superclass. This gives rise to a sort of family tree of classes, called the *inheritance hierarchy*. In the diagram below, class C inherits from (is a subclass of) class A, and is inherited by (is the superclass of) classes D, E, and F.

Instances of any particular class understand all the methods defined in their class, *and all the methods defined in their class's superclasses*. So an instance of class D would understand all the methods defined in D, C, A and so on up to the top of the tree. Just to confuse things further, if a method that an instance understands is actually defined in the instance's class (rather than in a superclass), the class is said to *implement* the method.

According to inheritance, instances of a class will contain all the instance variables defined in their class, *and all the instance variables defined in their class's superclasses*. So an instance of class G would have the instance variables defined in G, B, A and so on up to the top of the tree.

Note that normally you can make an instance of any class. In other words, it is not only those classes at the bottom of the hierarchy (the *leaves* of the tree) which can have instances. However, sometimes a programmer will design a class which is intended never to have instances. This doesn't mean it is useless though. It is there to collect together functionality which will be inherited by other classes which *will* have instances. Those classes which don't have instances are sometimes called *abstract* classes. In contrast, classes which are designed to have instances are called *concrete* classes.

A fragment of the class inheritance hierarchy showing how every class inherits from exactly one other class.

Is inherited by

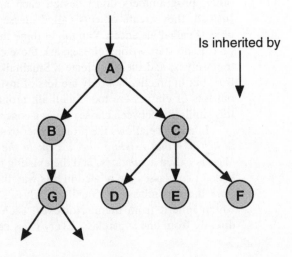

Over-riding and Polymorphism

Inheritance in Smalltalk can be thought of as *additive*. Each class inherits all the functionality of its superclass (and its superclass's superclass, and so on), and adds in some extra functionality (methods and variables) of its own. But what happens if a class attempts to add in some functionality which it is already inheriting? The answer depends on whether the class attempts to add methods or variables.

If a class attempts to define a new variable with the same name as a variable it inherits, the result is simply an error. In Smalltalk at least, there is no reason to want to redefine a variable lower down in an inheritance hierarchy.

However, if a class defines a new method with the same name as one it inherits, the new method replaces the inherited one in instances of that class, and its subclasses. The inherited method is said to be *over-ridden* by the definition lower down in the hierarchy. The original method doesn't go away. It still applies to instances of the class where it is defined, and instances of subclasses where it hasn't been over-ridden.

More generally, two different classes can define two different methods with the same name. This ability, together with the idea of being able to over-ride inherited method definitions, is a very powerful feature of object-oriented programming. It means that there can be all sorts of different method definitions with the same name. When a message is sent to an object naming a particular method, the actual method which is executed depends on the *class* of the object. This facility is called *polymorphism*. The reason this is such a powerful facility is that it allows different classes to define their own different ways of doing the same thing.

But how does the system find the right method to execute when a message is sent to an object? The answer is that it first looks in the class of which the object receiving the message is an instance. If there is a method with the right name there, that method is executed. If not, the system looks in the superclass. If it doesn't find the right method there, it looks in the superclass's superclass, and so on up to the top of the hierarchy. If the system reaches the top of the tree and still has not found a method with the right name, an error is generated.

This bottom-up searching process means that the method which is executed is always the one defined closest to the class of the object receiving the message. If you think about it, you'll see that this is how subclasses are able to over-ride the methods of their superclass.

Summary

This chapter has introduced all of the important concepts in object-oriented programming. We've seen that in OOP, *objects = code + data*. The data in an object is private to that object — a concept called *encapsulation*. Code is split into *methods*, which are invoked by sending *messages*. Objects are not defined individually, but by writing *classes*. Classes act as templates, and can also be thought of as factories for making *instances*. This process is called *instantiation*. Classes also share functionality with other classes using *inheritance*. Some classes are *abstract* (never having instances) and some are *concrete*. Finally, *over-riding* and *polymorphism* allow there to be more than one definition of a method.

It is useful to try to compare and contrast some of these concepts. In particular, it's important to remember the difference between a class and an instance. It's also useful to know the difference between *inheritance* and *instantiation*. (Inheritance is a relationship between classes, whereas instantiation is a relationship between an instance and its class.) Although it is tempting, it isn't quite correct to say that an instance inherits its functionality from its class. An instance gets its functionality from its class simply because it *is* an instance of that class.

As was suggested at the beginning of the chapter, all these concepts can seem a little strange at first. Don't worry if you haven't understood them perfectly. They will become clearer as you get more practical experience. Even if you have understood everything here, you are probably still left with the question 'How do I design my own objects, and how do I implement them in Smalltalk'? That is the question the rest of this book addresses.

An Introduction to Smalltalk

Now that we've looked at the general features of object-oriented programming, and explained some of the concepts and terminology involved, we can begin to look at the particular object-oriented language we're interested in—Smalltalk.

If you have previously programmed in a conventional language like C, Pascal, or COBOL, you'll be familiar with the process of creating a program. You'll be used to using a text editor to write your program, a compiler to compile it, a linker to link in any library routines you may have called and finally you'll be used to running it directly on your computer. You may also have used a debugger to debug your program. However, as you might have guessed by now, things are different in Smalltalk.

Smalltalk is a single, integrated system. It includes everything you need to develop, debug and run programs, all in one package. The purpose of this chapter is to explain what this means, and introduce the major parts of the system. The rest of Part I of the book is then structured according the notions introduced here.

The History of the Smalltalk System

Smalltalk was invented in the early 1970s at the Xerox Palo Alto Research Center (Xerox PARC) in California, USA. Originally a research system, it incorporated many new features, including the use of a window-based user-interface. Since there were none available at the time, Smalltalk implemented its own window system, the remnants of which are still visible today! It ran only on a Xerox computer.

Today, Smalltalk is an industry-standard, commercial and scientific language. There are a number of competing implementations available, running on a variety of platforms. Many of these systems are based on the Smalltalk-80 system from Xerox PARC. This book concentrates on one particular implementation of Smalltalk—*VisualWorks,* from ParcPlace Systems.

Structure of the Smalltalk System

The term *Smalltalk* is often used to refer to three distinct things: a programming language; a library of classes; and a development environment. Although conceptually separate, we shall see that these three things are actually highly interdependent. Every Smalltalk on the market, including *VisualWorks,* contains these three parts. There are differences between Smalltalks of course, but in general you will find that the actual languages are almost identical, the class libraries are somewhat similar, whilst the development environments are the most diverse. So, as the diagram over the page shows,

'Smalltalk' = a Language + a Class Library + a Development Environment

The Smalltalk *language* itself is very small. Compared to other languages like C, or even BASIC, there is almost nothing to it. Fundamentally, it allows you to define variables, assign objects to those variables and send messages to objects. Chapter 4 is devoted to a complete description of the Smalltalk language. You will see that unlike most other languages, it is relatively easy to know the entire Smalltalk language.

Almost everything in Smalltalk is an object (including numbers, strings, processes, *everything*), and almost everything (including arithmetic, tests, looping, input and output) is done by sending messages to objects. But the language itself does not define any of these objects or messages. Instead, all these things and many, many others are defined in the standard class library which accompanies the language.

The *class library* is the core of the Smalltalk system. It provides hundreds of reusable classes that you will use in each and every Smalltalk program you write. It also provides all the basic functionality you would normally think of as being part of a computer language. Because numbers are objects defined in the class library, arithmetic operations are done by sending messages to numbers. Because boolean

The three components of the
Smalltalk system.

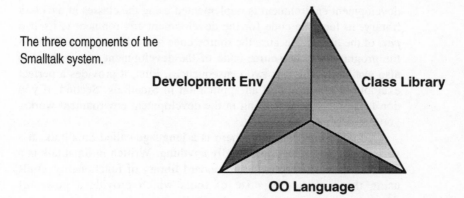

Development Env   **Class Library**

OO Language

values are also defined in the class library, conditional branches are done by sending messages to booleans. The class library contains objects which implement data structures that support looping (*collections*), and objects which provide input and output operations.

The Smalltalk class library is implemented using the Smalltalk language. It is built in the same way as you will build your own classes. Unlike the language itself though, the class library is very extensive. You could program in Smalltalk for years and never get to know the whole thing. This is not a problem though, because Smalltalk systems include *all the source-code* for the class library. This may seem like a dubious benefit. After all, the last thing most C programmers need or want is the source-code for the compiler (and, as we shall see, the editor, the debugger, the window system,...)! The presence of all this source-code makes large amounts of technicality frighteningly visible, but it also allows you to see precisely *how* the system works. If you can't remember what types of conditional branch are supported, you can look them up. If you need to understand some particular nuance of an operation in the class library, you can see *exactly* how it is implemented. Sounds frightening? Not so...

The source-code of the class library is made visible through the Smalltalk *development environment*. This consists of browsers, inspectors, debuggers, user-interface generators and a host of other tools. These tools can give a very clear view of how the system works—if you know how to use them. Much of this book is devoted to helping you in that respect. You use the development environment not only to look at the class library, but also to create, run and debug your own code. It is very rare in Smalltalk that you need to use a tool which is not provided as part of the development environment. The development environment is implemented using the classes in the class library. In fact, the code for the development environment is itself a *part* of the library. Because the source-code of the library is available to the programmer, the source-code of the development environment is also available. This has two consequences. First, it provides a perfect example of how to build an application in Smalltalk. Second, if you don't like the way something in the development environment works, you can in principle change it.

So what have we got? There is a language called Smalltalk. It's very small, and in fact does hardly anything. Written in Smalltalk is a set of classes which provide a standard library of functionality. Built using those classes is a set of tools which provide a powerful development environment for Smalltalk programmers. In a very real way, your task when programming in Smalltalk is to take that system, and extend it to turn it into what you want it to be. Unlike in other languages, there is no 'wall' between you and the system. You have all the same power and flexibility that the developers of the system itself enjoy.

Implementation of the Smalltalk System

When you program in C, Pascal, or many other languages, you usually think of your finished program as running straight on the hardware of your computer (albeit with the help of the operating system). Smalltalk however, introduces the concept of a *Virtual Machine* (VM) which sits between Smalltalk programs and the actual computer. You can think of this virtual machine as a sort of idealised Smalltalk computer, on which both the Smalltalk development tools, and your Smalltalk programs run. The VM works in association with a *Virtual Image* (VI, or just the *image*). You can think of the image as being equivalent to the memory of the virtual machine. The image is where the development tools, the Smalltalk code-library and your programs actually reside. The diagram on the next page shows this structure.

Isolating Smalltalk programs from the hardware of the computer is what enables Smalltalk to be so incredibly portable across different platforms. Each different platform (workstation, PC, Macintosh, etc.) has its own version of the VM in the form of an executable file. However, because it's the same virtual computer that's being implemented by the VM, the *identical* image file will run on any implementation of the VM. To port your program between platforms

Smalltalk Virtual Image

VisualWorks Development Environment

Your Classes
(All your application's code)

Class Library
(Numbers, Strings, Collections,
Views, Widgets...)

(Tools, Browsers, Inspectors, Editors, Debuggers...)

Smalltalk Virtual Machine

Your Computer
(Workstation, PC, Mac...)

The Smalltalk system
consists of a *virtual image*
and a *virtual machine*
running on your computer.

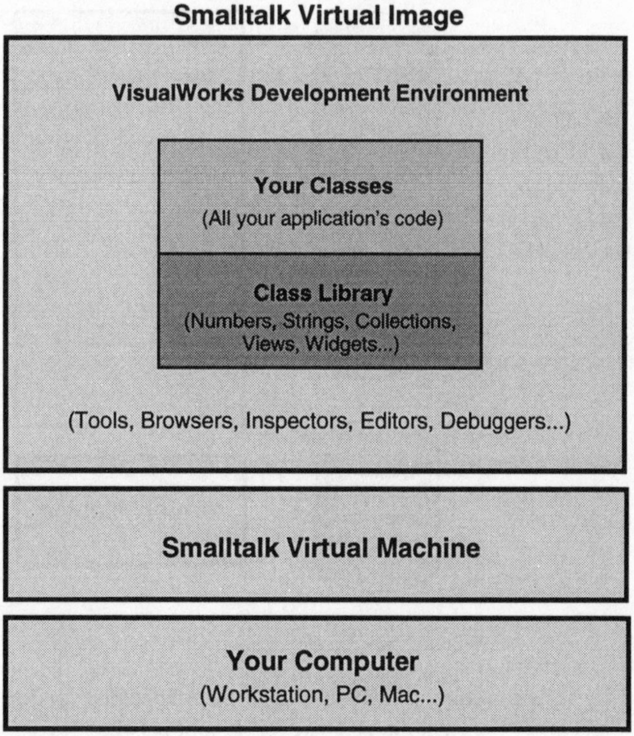

you simply the copy the image! To achieve this consistency, the VM
implements its own set of basic operations, including arithmetic, logical
and I/O operations. These operations are translated into the operations
your computer is actually capable of at run-time. Originally this was
accomplished by an interpreter, but in *VisualWorks* at least, this is now
done by an incremental compiler to give faster code.

Files the System Lives In

The Smalltalk system as described above lives in a number of different
files. These are shown in the diagram over the page. It is very helpful to
have a clear understanding of what these different files are, as not only
do they hold the system, they hold your programs too.

The virtual machine is an executable program in whatever format
your computer supports. As such it lives in its own file, usually called

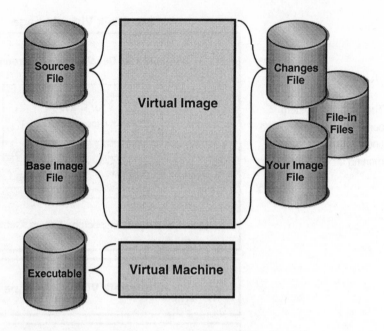

The Smalltalk VM, VI, source-code and your code is held in number of files.

oe20 (or **st80** if you have an older version of *VisualWorks*). The virtual image however, is split between several files of different types.

The most important type of file is the *image file*. This is a snapshot in binary form of all the code and data in the virtual image at a particular time. Because they contain the entire image, image files are typically several megabytes in size. *VisualWorks* comes with a standard 'base' image file containing the entire class library and the development environment. This is typically called something like **visual.im**. When you start *VisualWorks*, the VM loads the image file into the memory of your computer where it can be worked on. As you program, the image in memory is changing all the time. You can save it back to a file (using a name to which the system will add **.im**) whenever you wish, thus creating your own image file. Because the image file contains *everything* in the image, if you restart *VisualWorks* using one of your image files you will recreate the entire state of the environment at the time you saved it, including windows open, programs running, etc. This is a very useful feature. Provided you have enough disk-space, you should save your image frequently (at least every 30 minutes or whenever you make a serious change), as it is a very convenient way of storing your work.

One thing that is *not* stored in image files though, is source-code. This applies both to the source of the class library, and the source of your programs. The source-code of the standard class library (in other words, the source-code for the base image file) is held in the *sources* file. This is a text file (although you wouldn't normally read it yourself), which may be called **visual.sources**. The system does not load up the entire sources file when it starts. Instead, it goes to it each time it needs to get the source of a particular method for you to look at. The source-code is not needed for the method to run. In fact, the system will run quite happily without the sources file—you just won't be able to browse the code very well.

The source-code for the classes and methods you write is not held in the sources file. Instead, it is held in the *changes* file. This is a text file which holds all the source-code for all the changes and additions *you* have made to the image. There is typically one changes file for each image file, usually called **<name>.changes** (**.cha** on the PC) where **<name>** is whatever name you gave to your image file. Together, the sources file and the changes file hold all the source-code for the image.

Just like the sources files, the changes file is not loaded up in its entirety when *VisualWorks* is started. Instead the system goes to it each time it needs the source-code for one of your methods. *Unlike* the sources file though, which is never written to, the changes file is written to every time you modify anything in the system. This happens all the time, not just when you save your image. Also, a new version of a method does not overwrite the old version in the changes file. It is simply added onto the end. This means that the changes file is building up a complete *history* of the changes and additions you've made to the system. *VisualWorks* provides some tools that allow you to use this to recover from crashes or revert to previous versions of your code.

The final kind of file that is of interest to us here is the *file-in* file. We've mentioned that it's possible to save your work by saving the entire image in an image file. This is a very convenient way of creating a snapshot of the entire state of the system, but not a very convenient way of saving smaller pieces of code, perhaps to give to someone else. To cater for this, *VisualWorks* provides a *file-out* mechanism which will write out just the code you ask for to a separate file. The resulting file can be *filed-in* to another image. File-ins are text-files holding Smalltalk source-code, although you would not normally edit them outside the *VisualWorks* system. You can use file-ins to share code amongst several developers. They are also very important if you need to rebuild your image from the base image—something which can happen if your image becomes corrupted. It is a very good idea to file-out your code regularly (whenever it is in a stable state), as well as saving your image.

Summary

Smalltalk is a self-contained system consisting of a language, a class library and a development environment. These three things are all contained in something called a virtual image, which runs on top of the Smalltalk virtual machine, which in turn is an executable program running on your computer. The whole virtual image can be saved in a file and restored later. Your code lives inside the image, or in file-in files you create.

Programming in Smalltalk consists of using the Smalltalk language and development environment to extend the class library to make it do the things you want it to do. We'll come to that very soon. The next step is to look at the specifics of the Smalltalk language.

The Smalltalk Language

Smalltalk, true to its name, is a very small language. There really is very little to it. All the power (and complexity) of Smalltalk comes from the large class library, and the extensive development environment. We'll be looking at the class library and the development environment in later chapters. This chapter is about Smalltalk—the language. Here we'll explain the basic constructions which are used to declare variables, assign values, send messages, and so on. These are the nuts and bolts of Smalltalk programming, and the building blocks of methods and classes. Later on we'll look at how to use these building blocks to understand the system code, and define your own methods and classes.

Naming Conventions

Before looking at the actual Smalltalk language it's useful to mention a piece of style advice. Smalltalk programmers usually follow a strict convention when naming classes, variables, and methods. All these things can have names which consist of multiple English words. The words are simply joined together, with a capital letter at the start of each new word. Smalltalkers don't tend to use underscores (_) to separate words. Whether a name starts with an upper- or lower-case letter depends on the kind of thing it is naming—we'll mention each special case as we go along. Here are some example Smalltalk names:

height schoolHistory ControllerWithMenu anOrderedCollection

Look at the last one—**anOrderedCollection**. It is an example of a very common naming convention in Smalltalk. If there is no better name for a variable, it is usually named after its class, with a prefix of '**a**' or '**an**'. Long names are perfectly acceptable. In fact, they're encouraged because they make your code easier to read, and hence easier to reuse. Just as in all languages, the more descriptive you can make your names, the better.

Literals and Constants

Smalltalk provides a number of different sorts of *literal*. These are things like numbers and strings which you can include freely in programs just by typing them. Here are some Smalltalk numbers:

```
123      3.14      2.789e31      22/7      -0.07
```

Notice that Smalltalk can handle integers, floating point numbers, and slightly unusually, fractions. You need to be aware of this because if a fraction is the most accurate way of representing a number, that is what Smalltalk will do unless you ask otherwise. This can sometimes be a little confusing if you need to look at the numbers your program is using, especially during debugging.

Smalltalk strings are enclosed in single quotes ('). Any character at all is permitted inside a string, but if you need to include a single quote you'll need to use two of them. Don't make the mistake of trying to put strings inside double quotes ("). Smalltalk uses those to delimit comments! Here are some example strings, and an example comment:

```
'Apple'
'Peter''s Pepper'
'This is a Smalltalk string.'
"And this is a Smalltalk comment!"
```

As in other languages, strings are used frequently in Smalltalk. Less frequently, you'll need to deal with individual character objects as literals. These are specified by prefixing the character with a **$** symbol. For example: **$a**, **$z**, **$<**. Remember that a string with one character in it *is a different object* to the character itself. That is, '**f**' is not the same as **$f**.

Smalltalk also provides objects called *symbols*. These are similar to strings except that they are unique. This means that whilst you could create several *string* objects containing the same sequence of characters, there will only be exactly one instance of a *symbol* with a given sequence of characters. This makes them more efficient for their intended use—naming objects and states. Their use is very much a matter of style and will become clear as we go on. If you are used to enumerated types or #defines in C, you will find the way symbols are usually used in Smalltalk very familiar. Here are some example symbols:

#red   #syndicateList   #waiting

As we shall discuss in detail later, the Smalltalk class library contains many different sorts of collection object. However one of them, the array of literals, can itself be created literally. Here is an example:

#(2 7.59 'Hello' #resetPending)

This example creates an array of four other objects—two numbers, a string, and a symbol. Notice how all these objects are literals. Don't try to put anything more complex in one of these arrays—it won't work. We'll learn how to make more general collections of any object in the chapter on collections.

Finally, there are three special *constant*s in Smalltalk: **true**, **false**, and **nil**. Whenever you refer to one of these, you are actually referring to objects which are the sole instances of the classes **True**, **False**, and **UndefinedObject** respectively. Obviously **true** and **false** are used to represent boolean states, whilst **nil** is used to represent the notion of 'nothing' or 'undefined'. As with many things in this chapter, this will become clear as you get more experience!

Variables

Smalltalk is often described as being 'typeless'. Confusingly, this doesn't mean there aren't any types. Every object in the system has a type, or in Smalltalk terminology, a class. For example, there are objects which are integers, strings, arrays, files, windows, and so on. What is meant is that Smalltalk *variables* are typeless.

Just as in other languages, Smalltalk variables have a name and a value. The name can be almost anything, subject to a few conventions. The value can be *any object*. So, if you have a variable called **origin** for example, it can hold a floating point number, or a date, or a menu, or any other kind of Smalltalk object. As in other languages you still have to *declare* the variable, but all you have to do is give it a name, not a type. You don't need to say 'Give me a variable called **age** of type **integer**.' You just say 'Give me a variable called **age**.'

This typelessness can seem very distressing at first, and even unsafe. In fact, it is a key contributor to the flexibility and power of

Smalltalk code. It facilitates the use of the *polymorphism* we looked at in Chapter 2, and really doesn't cause the kind of bugs you might imagine. Stick with it—you'll come to love the power it gives!

We usually talk about an object being 'in' a variable if the variable's value is that object. Sometimes though it's more convenient to talk about a variable being 'a pointer to' an object. These two concepts are the same thing. Unlike C, Smalltalk does not have (or need) the notion of pointers. If it helps to think of it this way, remember that everything in Smalltalk is *passed by reference*.

There are six kinds of variable in Smalltalk: temporary; instance; class; class–instance; global; and pool. Each kind of variable has a different scope and lifetime, and is declared in a different way. When declared they are initialised to a special value called **nil**. Whether you choose to use this fact, or start your code by setting new variables to another value is a matter of programming style and is up to you. Now let's look at the different variables one by one:

Temporary Variables

These have the smallest scope and the shortest lifetime. They are declared within a single method and are only visible within that method. They last only as long as the method execution—their value is not preserved across multiple executions. You can think of them as being like the 'local' variables in other languages. By convention, their names start with a lower-case letter. Temporaries are declared all together at the beginning of each method in which they are going to be used. This is done by just naming them between a pair of vertical bars (||). For example:

```
| size qualityOfLife ambition |
```

would declare three variables called **size**, **qualityOfLife**, and **ambition**. Notice how the variables are not given a 'type'. They can all hold objects of any class. These variables are now declared for the duration of the method, and will be initialised to **nil**.

Instance Variables

These are the kind of variables we thought of as being *encapsulated* in every object in Chapter 2. They are private to the object, but visible to all the methods of that object. Instance variables exist and keep their values for as long as their containing object exists. This might be a very short time, or very long time, depending entirely on the object in question. They are declared in the *class* of the object using one of the browsers which are part of the development environment. We'll look at browsers later. Remember that every instance of a class has its own copy of the instance variables defined in the class. They have the same names, but different values. Instance variable names always start with a lower-case letter.

Class Variables

Class variables are similar to instance variables except that they exist only in classes. They are visible to the class itself, and to every instance of the class. Unlike instance variables though, every instance sees *the same variable*. This allows data to be shared amongst all instances of a class and its subclasses. Class variable names start with an upper-case letter.

Class–Instance Variables

Variables of this kind are only directly accessible by a class (and not by its instances). Their value is not shared down the inheritance hierarchy. Like class variables, they start with an upper-case letter. They are confusingly named and very rarely used, so if the following example doesn't make sense, come back to it if you ever think you need to use a class–instance variable.

Imagine there is a class called **A** with two subclasses called **B** and **C**. Class **A** defines one *class* variable, one *instance* variable, and one *class–instance* variable. Given this definition, the following will apply:

Classes **A**, **B**, and **C**, and every instance of **A**, **B**, and **C** will *share* the same *class* variable. Every instance of **A**, **B** and **C** will have its own *private* copy of the *instance* variable. Classes **A**, **B** and **C** will each have its own *private class–instance* variable. In other words, there will be exactly one copy of the class variable, as many copies of the instance variable as there are instances, and as many copies of the class–instance variable as there are classes (three in this case). Remember, instance variables are visible only to instances, class variables to classes *and* instances, and class–instance variables only to classes. Yes, it *is* confusing!

Global Variables

Smalltalk global variables are just like globals in other languages. They are declared once (either interactively when first referenced, or by sending a message to an object called **Smalltalk**), persist 'for ever' and are visible everywhere. By convention their names always start with an upper-case letter. Provided you are careful, you should feel free to use global variables. All class names in the system are actually global variables, and there are several other important system globals around. You should be careful not to assign anything to these as the results will be unpredictable at minimum!

Pool variables

These are similar to global variables except that their scope is restricted to the particular set of classes which the programmer has permitted to access them. This makes them more flexible than class variables, but less dangerous than globals. They are grouped together into 'dictionaries' which define sets of pool variables.

Here is an example class definition (for a class called **Square**) which defines two instance variables (**size** and **colour**), one class variable (**Material**), and one pool dictionary (**Shapes**). Don't worry about the syntax of the definition for now—we'll cover that in the next chapter.

```
Object subclass: #Square
    instanceVariableNames: 'size colour'
    classVariableNames: 'Material'
    poolDictionaries: 'Shapes'
```

Special or Psuedo-Variables

There are two so-called psuedo-variables in Smalltalk: **self** and **super**. These are not true variables because you cannot directly assign anything to them. However, they are not constants because their values vary depending on the context in which they are used.

When the psuedo-variable **self** appears in a method, it means 'me'. The only way a method can be invoked is by sending a message. So, if a method in an object wants to invoke another of the object's own methods (a very common occurrence actually), it has to send a message to itself. To enable it to do that, it can refer to itself as **self**.

Similar to **self** is **super**. When an object sends a message to **super**, it is saying in effect 'I don't want to invoke my own definition of this method, I want to invoke my superclass's definition.' This is useful so that inheritance and over-riding can be used to *extend* a superclass's method in a subclass, instead of just to *replace* it. In other words, a subclass would define a method with the same name as a method in its superclass. This method might call the superclass's method (using **super**) and then do some extra processing itself.

Sending Messages

Almost everything in Smalltalk is done by sending a message to an object. This is done by first naming the object, and then the message. If the method being invoked needs some parameters, they can be sent too. Smalltalk has a special way of sending parameters by embedding them inside method names. Here are some example (fictional) message sends:

```
MyStorageSystem initialize.
aSquare increaseSizeBy: 34.
manager employ: 'Aristotle' as: 'philosopher'.
Database open: 'people.dat' using: key rwMode: 7.
```

We're not interested in what these messages actually accomplish (don't try them, because unless you've created them they won't be in your system!). We're interested in the structure of the message expressions. To help you understand them, we'll compare them to the same sort of expressions in a procedural language such as C, BASIC, Pascal or COBOL. Smalltalk does not support this procedural syntax, so feel free to ignore it if it does not help.

The first example is simple. It sends the message **initialize** to the object called **MyStorageSystem**. You can't tell from this code fragment but **MyStorageSystem** is probably a global variable. Provided the object in this variable has a method called **initialize**, it will run it. If you're used to procedural programming, you can think of this as being somewhat like calling the procedure **initialize**, which takes no parameters—**initialize()**. The only difference is that in object-oriented programming, there could be lots of different implementations of **initialize**. The one which is actually run depends on the the the class of **MyStorageSystem**.

In the second example an object called **aSquare** (probably an instance variable or temporary variable) is being sent the message **increaseSizeBy:** with a parameter, **34**. Note the colon (**:**) at the end of the message name. This is a part of the message name, and specifies that a parameter is coming. It's important to remember that the colon is a part of the message name, and not just an extra bit of syntax like the parentheses in a procedure call. To emphasise this, Smalltalkers pronounce the colon when talking about a method—'increase-size-by-colon'. Two methods with identical names except for a colon (like **colour** and **colour:**) are two *different* methods. One takes a parameter and one does not. They could be defined to do two completely different things. The procedural equivalent of this message expression would be **increaseSizeBy(34)**, although again remember that in OOP there could be lots of different versions of **increaseSizeBy:**.

The third example is where things get interesting. Here an object called manager is being sent a message with two parameters: **'Aristotle'** and **'philosopher'**. The method name is **employ:as:** (pronounced 'employ-colon-as-colon'). Notice how the parameters are embedded into the method name to make up the message. This is an unusual feature of Smalltalk, but can make expressions read very clearly (although you may not agree at first!). The procedural equivalent of this method would be something like **employAs('philosopher', 'Aristotle')**.

The last example just shows how this embedding of parameters can be extended to as many parameters as the method requires. In this case the method **open:using:rwMode:** takes three parameters: the string **'people.dat'**; **key** (which is a variable); and **7**. The equivalent expression in a procedural language would be something like **openUsingrwMode('people.dat', key, 7)**.

Notice that each of the example message sends above ended with a full-stop (**.**) or period character. This is always necessary in Smalltalk if there are further message expressions to be evaluated, in order to separate one expression from the next. It is optional if there are no further message expressions being evaluated (for example, at the end of a method, or at the end of a single line of code being executed interactively).

Assignment

In Smalltalk, every message expression has a *value*. Executing a message expression (or *evaluating* it, in Smalltalk-speak) causes a method to be run. Every method returns an object when it finishes. This returned object is then referred to as the value of the expression. Sometimes the writer of the method will have specified explicitly what to return. This is done using an up-arrow or caret (**^**) character. For example, the expression **^true** in a method would cause the method to terminate, returning the value **true**. Other methods might not include a **^**. In these cases the system just runs them to completion, and then returns **self** —the receiver or object which was sent the message.

The return value of a message may be assigned to a variable using the operator **:=**. Some programmers call this operator 'becomes', 'gets', or just 'colon-equals'. Here are some (fictional) examples:

```
Total := net + tax.
aForm := Form with: people size: 15.
MyObject := YourObject.
```

In the first example, the values of **net** and **tax** are added together, and the result is assigned to **Total**. In the second example, the result of sending the message **with:size:** to **Form** is assigned to **aForm**. We shall see later that this is actually the sort of expression used to make new instances.

The third example is there to remind us of something very important. The **:=** operator does not make a copy of the object being assigned. If **YourObject** contains a particular object, then after the third example is evaluated **MyObject** will contain *the same object*. In other words, there will be one object 'pointed to' by two variables: **MyObject** and **YourObject**. Usually this is exactly the intended effect. However, it can give rise to some very nasty bugs if you forget that both variables contain the same object! If you try to treat them as separate objects, and change one of them (for example **MyObject**), you'll be very surprised when the other object (**YourObject**) changes too! Bugs like this can take a long time to track down, so take care. Note that assigning a new object to one of the variables (doing something like **MyObject := 'Hello'**) does not change the other variable, which remains 'pointing to' the previous object.

Combining Messages

The fact that every message expression has a value means that messages can be combined in several useful ways. For example, one message can follow on after another. In this case the second message is sent to the object which is the result of the first message. Here is an example:

```
aTriangle height asInteger.
```

In this case the message **height** is sent to **aTriangle**, and then the message **asInteger** is sent to whatever object is returned by the message **height**. This sort of construction is called *chaining*. If you like to think in procedural terms you can imagine this as being similar to **asInteger(height(aTriangle))**.

Notice how the example expression is executed from left to right. This is not always the case. Smalltalk has some slightly unusual precedence rules which govern the order in which expressions are evaluated. These seem peculiar at first but rapidly become second nature:

Message expressions are divided into three types: *unary*—those which take no parameters; *binary*—for example **+, *, > =**; and *keyword*—those which take one or more parameters after colons in the method name. In a complex expression, unary messages are evaluated first. If there is more than one, they are executed from left to right. Binary messages are evaluated next, again from left to right. Finally, keyword messages are evaluated, also from left to right. Just as in other languages, parentheses can be used to change the order of evaluation. In this case the expression in the inner-most parentheses is evaluated first (according to normal Smalltalk rules). Here are some examples:

```
MyCollection add: Pyramid new initialize.
(book openAtPage: 1+2*3) print.
(agenda item:7) title: 'Plans'.
```

In the first case the message **new** is sent to **Pyramid**. The resulting object is sent the message **initialize**. The object which is returned by **initialize** is then used as a parameter in the message **add:** sent to **MyCollection**. Notice how the unary messages (**new** and **initialize**) were evaluated first (from left to right), and then the keyword message (**add:**).

In the second example the contents of the parentheses are evaluated first. There are two binary messages (**+** and *****) and one keyword message (**openAtPage:**) in the parentheses. The binary messages are evaluated first, which working from left to right gives a value of **9** (not **7** as in normal arithmetical precedence!). Then the message **openAtPage:9** is sent to **book**, and finally whatever object that message returns is sent the message **print**. Note that without the parantheses the order would have been different. The system would have started by sending the message **print** to **3**. It would then have added **1** and **2** and tried to multiply the result by whatever was returned from sending **print** to **3**. This would probably result in an error!

The third example illustrates that parentheses are frequently needed even if we want the expression to be evaluated straight from left to right. In this case we want the message **item:7** to be sent to

agenda, and then have the *resulting object* sent the message **title:'Plans'** . Without the parentheses, the system would send the message **item:7 title:'Plans'** to agenda, which is not the same thing at all (because it is trying to invoke the single method **item:title:** and not the separate methods **item:** and **title:**). This confusion arises because of the way Smalltalk embeds parameters within method names.

The second way of combining messages in Smalltalk is called *cascading*. When messages are cascaded, each one is followed by a semicolon (;) and another message. In this case, subsequent messages are sent to the *first* receiver, and not as in chaining, to the object *returned* from the first message. Consider the difference between these two message expressions:

```
diskController reset initialize startRunning.
diskController reset; initialize; startRunning.
```

In the first case (chaining), the **diskController** is sent the message **reset** . Then the *object which was returned* from that message is sent the message **initialize** . Then the *object which was returned* by **initialize** is sent the message **startRunning**. In the second case (cascading) the **diskController** is sent the message **reset**. Then **diskController** is sent **initialize**, followed by **startRunning**. If **reset** and **initialize** return **self** (in this case **diskController**) then these two expressions are identical. If **reset** and **initialize** return anything other than **self** then these two expressions are definitely not identical. Think about it...

Of the two message combining techniques (chaining and cascading), chaining—the one without the semicolons—is by far the more common, being used almost everywhere. Cascading is much rarer, partly because in many places where you might use it, the methods return **self** anyway (by default if nothing else) and so chaining can be used instead. It's as well to remember about cascading though, as you will see it in the system code, and may sometimes find it useful in your own code.

Primitive Operations

As you are browsing around the methods in the Smalltalk class library you will occasionally come across expressions which look like this:

```
<primitive: 63>
```

These are calls to the primitive operations (or just *primitives*) which the virtual machine itself supports. Typically they are used to do very low-level operations, and you can usually guess what from the name of the method involved. The code which follows these expressions in a method is only executed if the primitive fails. Only if you are adding user-defined primitives in order to call out to other languages will you need to actually write these expressions. Otherwise, there is little you can do but ignore them when you come across them.

Blocks of Code

The last piece of the Smalltalk language we need to look at here is the notion of *blocks*. We have already looked at how Smalltalk code is written in chunks called *methods*. These methods are defined in classes and executed by send messages to instances of those classes. They are, in a sense, bound to the objects which define them. It is also possible however, to define chunks of Smalltalk code called blocks. These pieces of code are not associated with a particular class, but are objects in their own right. They can be created at run-time, passed around, executed one or more times and thrown away.

Blocks (implemented by the class **BlockClosure**) are a very powerful feature of Smalltalk, but one which has no direct analogy in many other languages. If you are used to programming in C though, you can think of blocks as being *used* somewhat like pointers to functions. However, we won't look at how they are used here—that's covered later. We'll just look at how they are created and executed. Notice that the creation of a block object is a separate thing from its execution. In a sense, blocks represent a form of *deferred* execution. Here are three example blocks:

```
aBlock := [Recycler initialize].

MyBlock := [:anObject | anObject print].

anotherBlock := [:parm1 :parm2 | | temp |
            temp := parm1 incorporate: parm2.
            temp rehash.
            ].
```

The first example creates a simple block which *when executed* will send the message **initialize** to **Recycler**. The block (not the value it returns, but the block of code *itself*) is put in a variable called

aBlock. The second example creates a block and puts it in a variable called **MyBlock**. The block itself takes one parameter (**anObject**, preceded by a colon and followed by a |). The block has not been executed yet, but when it is it will send the message **print** to whatever parameter it is passed. The third example creates a block which takes two parameters and also defines a temporary variable called **temp** (between the pair of | 's). Like all these examples, don't worry about what this block might *do*, just look at how it's constructed.

That's how blocks are created. Now let's take a look at how they're actually *executed*. There are in fact a number of different ways of executing blocks—the simplest being to send them a variant of the message **value**. For example:

```
MyBlock value:
     'This string will be sent the message print'.
```

Blocks can actually take anything from zero to 255 arguments. Different versions of the 'value' message must be used depending on the number of arguments. Here are the variants:

value   for no arguments,

value: anObject   for one argument,

value: object1 value: object2   for two arguments,

value: obj1 value: obj2 value: obj3   ...three arguments,

valueWithArguments: argArray   ...more than three arguments.

Very often though, you won't actually send **value** (or **value :**, etc.) to the blocks you create—it'll be done by the object you pass the block on to. We'll see plenty of examples of this later in the book. The other ways of executing blocks include some which have the effect of implementing control structures, and others which allow you to 'spawn off' separate processes inside Smalltalk.

Summary

We've now covered the entire Smalltalk language by looking at the naming conventions and describing literals, constants, variables, pseudo-variables, assignment, message expressions and blocks. That really is all there is to it.

At this point you may be puzzled as to why we haven't looked at class definitions, arithmetic, input/output, control structures and so on.

In fact, these things are not a part of the language, but are implemented (along with thousands of other operations) in the Smalltalk class library. This means that unlike in most other languages, their definitions are available for you to see and understand on-line. This is a very useful feature, which saves you from having to consult the manual too frequently when you want to know *exactly* what a basic operation will do.

Of course, you do need to have some idea of what kinds of operation exist, and so we'll summarize them in Chapter 6—*The Smalltalk Class Library* and then look in more detail at these types of operation as we come across them all in later chapters. Before that, the next chapter introduces the way in which you can look at source-code in the system, and develop your own programs by using the Smalltalk development environment.

The Smalltalk Development Environment

In chapter 3 we discussed how the term *Smalltalk* applies to three different things: an object-oriented language; an application development environment; and a standard class library. Having introduced the Smalltalk language we are now ready to look at the second part of this trilogy—the development environment.

The Smalltalk development environment is your window on the Smalltalk virtual image introduced in chapter 3. Remember that the virtual image includes all the classes, instances, windows and everything else in the Smalltalk system. The development environment provides many different kinds of tool which enable you to see and modify these things. Exactly which tools you have available depends on the version of Smalltalk you have, and whether you have any optional, add-on tools. This chapter will focus on the core tools used to develop Smalltalk programs—tools which should be available in all Smalltalk environments. We won't be looking specifically at the *VisualWorks* user-interface development tools.

Because Smalltalk is an integrated system, you should never find it necessary to use tools outside the development environment, for example to edit code or debug your application. Unlike other languages, you don't type Smalltalk code into a file using a text-editor, and then 'compile' it. The only exception to this rule is if you are particularly concerned with connecting Smalltalk to code written in another language. Otherwise, you should find that all your code development, testing and debugging can be done interactively inside the development environment. This even applies to printing things out, which is far less useful in Smalltalk than it is in other languages. Too much of the meaning of Smalltalk code is embodied in its *structure*, which is lost when you print it out.

The Different Kinds of Tool

At the highest level, the tools in the development environment can be divided into a number of different types. There are tools which allow you to see and write Smalltalk classes (*browsers*). There are tools which allow you to see and modify Smalltalk instances (*inspectors*). There are tools which help you to test and debug Smalltalk code (*workspaces, notifiers, debuggers*). You can look at files (*file list* and *file editor* tools), and manage changes to your image (*change list*). Finally, the *VisualWorks* environment also provides many tools for developing graphical user-interfaces (GUIs), and connecting to relational databases.

You will find yourself using some of these tools more than others, but it's important to remember that the others are there when you need them. Also, remember that you can usually open as many of each tool as you need (screen space permitting of course). Don't struggle along with just a single browser for example, if you really need three or four (or ten!) open.

Because this is a book on *Smalltalk*, we'll concentrate here mainly on the tools used to create, edit and debug Smalltalk code, rather than on the GUI or database connectivity tools. Once you have an understanding of these basic tools, you should find it easy to work out how to use the others, either by reading the manual, or simply by exploring the system. The aim of this chapter is to make sure you have at least a basic understanding of the tools. A subsequent chapter in Part II—*The Art of Smalltalk* describes in detail how to make really effective use of them.

Using the Mouse

Traditionally, Smalltalk uses a three-button mouse. Your *physical* mouse may have only one or two buttons, but *logically* Smalltalk binds three different functions to the mouse. Your system documentation will tell you how to simulate three buttons by using various combinations of shift key. In the very beginning these buttons were named after colours, and you may in fact still see them referred to in that way in the depths of the system code or comments. These days the Smalltalk manuals refer to the buttons as the *select*, *operate* and *window* buttons.

The *select* button (left button on workstations and PCs; the one and only mouse button on a Macintosh; 'red' button in the old days) is used as its name suggests, to select things in the Smalltalk environment. You

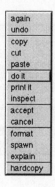

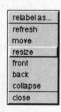

Typical *operate* (on left) and
window (on right) menus.

can click on things like radio buttons, check boxes or items in lists, or
you can press and drag in the usual way to select pieces of text.
Double-clicking the button will select a single word in a text window,
or the whole of the text if you're at the very top left of the window

The *operate* button (middle button on workstations; right button on
PCs; option-mouse button on a Macintosh; 'yellow' button in the old
days) is used to pop up a menu (see diagram above). The menu you get
will depend on where the mouse pointer is. This can be very
specific—different parts of a single window will give you different
menus when you use the *operate* button in them. These menus contain
commands which are relevant in the context of the particular window
(and part of the window) the pointer is in. These commands are in fact
one of the main ways of interacting with the Smalltalk system.

The *window* button (right button on workstations; control-right
button on a PC; command-mouse button on a Macintosh; 'blue' button
in the old days) is left over from from the days when Smalltalk was
itself a window system running straight on the operating system of the
computer. Pressing it will pop up a menu (see diagram above)
containing all the familiar window management functions of move,
resize, close and so on. If you wish, you can ignore this button and use
the window management facilities provided by your window system
(MS Windows, X, Macintosh or whatever). Sometimes though, you
may find that it's rather more convenient to be able to access the
window menu from Smalltalk—it's your choice. The only important
thing to remember is that if you find yourself looking at a menu full of
window management functions when you wanted a menu of more
useful things, you're probably pressing the wrong mouse button!

41

The combined launcher and transcript window of *VisualWorks* 2.0 (front) and separate Launcher and Transcript windows from an earlier version (behind).

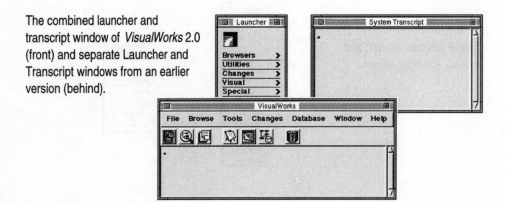

The Launcher and Transcript

The *Launcher* is really the root of the development environment. All of the major tools can be opened (or launched) from the menu it provides (although some of the other tools can only be started in the context in which they are used—it should usually be obvious where). The launcher's menu also allows you to save your work by saving the virtual image into a file on disk. This is certainly something you should do very frequently!

The *Transcript* is a text window in which the system reports important events. You can also print things in the transcript window (perhaps for debugging purposes) using an expression such as:

```
Transcript show: 'A message to the transcript'.
```

The global variable **Transcript** actually contains an instance of the class **TextCollector**, so browsing that class (we'll see exactly how later of you're unsure) will tell you about all the other things you can do with the transcript.

Depending on the version of *VisualWorks* you are using, the launcher and the transcript window(s) may look different. They may in fact be in two different windows, or they may be combined into a single window. The diagram above shows both kinds. Either way, the basic functionality and purpose of each tool is the same.

A typical workspace window about to
evaluate a Smalltalk expression.

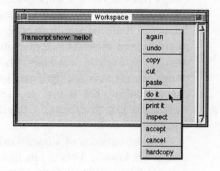

Workspaces

Workspaces, like the one shown above, are your scratchpad. You can
type pieces of Smalltalk code into a workspace and execute them
immediately. Note that you can't define Smalltalk *classes* in a
workspace (that happens in a *browser*), but you can define global and
temporary variables, send messages to objects and look at the results.
This is a very useful facility which you should find invaluable for
experimenting with the system code, and for testing your own code.

If you type a Smalltalk expression into a workspace (anything will
do, even something as simple as **1+1**), select it using the *select* mouse
button so that it is highlighted, and then press the *operate* mouse
button, you will see a menu which is very common throughout the
development environment. There are three important commands in the
middle of this menu—**do it**; **print it**; and **inspect** (it). All these three
commands allow you to execute (or *evaluate* in Smalltalk-speak) the
Smalltalk expression you have got selected. The first command, **do it**,
simply evaluates the expression and throws the result away. This is
useful if you want the side-effect of the expression but are not
interested in the return value. The second command, **print it**, does
exactly what **do it** does, but it also prints the result in the workspace
window. This is useful if you wish to see the result, but it does corrupt
the workspace with extra text (although note that this is conveniently
highlighted for you to delete it with the backspace key). The third
command, **inspect** (for some reason the 'it' is missing), also does
exactly what **do it** does, but it opens an *inspector* window on the object
returned by the expression. We'll be looking at inspectors shortly.

You may find it useful to keep several workspaces open containing
bits of code on which you are working. Also, note that the kind of

things you can do in a workspace (**do it**; **print it**; **inspect**) you can also do in *almost every* Smalltalk window. This is an extremely useful facility as it allows you to execute little snippets of code wherever you might happen to be. This applies in the transcript, browsers, inspectors, debuggers, even in windows which you yourself create. Of course, things can get very untidy if you go typing random bits of Smalltalk in every window, but it can be useful not to have to find or open a workspace just to execute a single line. Just type it in any window, select it, and **do it**.

Earlier versions of *VisualWorks* also provided something called a *system workspace*. This is just like an ordinary workspace, except that it is pre-filled with all sorts of useful code fragments for you to use. There is also the *installation workspace* which again is just a workspace that happens to be filled with code to do with 'installing' *VisualWorks* on your system. If you happen to be using one of these earlier versions, and if all you want is a plain workspace, be careful that that is what you ask for from the launcher.

Browsers

If you're familiar with conventional programming in which you use a text-editor to write your code and save it in files, you have probably been wondering where exactly you write Smalltalk classes. Here is the answer. The tools used for this purpose are called *browsers*. A browser

Categories   Classes   Protocols   Methods

A system browser browsing the category **Kernel-Objects**, class **Object**, protocol **printing** and method **print String**.

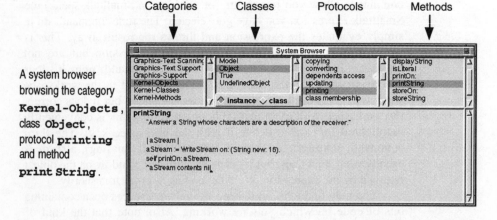

allows you to look at the source-code of a class, examine its methods and create, modify or delete both classes and methods. The development environment provides many different kinds of browser but they all have a lot of features in common. We'll look mainly at just one kind of browser—the *system browser*.

The diagram on page 44 shows a system browser being used to examine the source-code of a class (the class **Object** in this case). To understand how it works it is necessary to understand a few things about how the Smalltalk development environment organises classes and methods for browsing purposes.

To make it easier to manage the hundreds of classes in the class hierarchy, they are grouped together into groups called *categories*. Each category contains classes which are related in terms of their purpose. It's important to realise that categories have nothing to do with inheritance. Categories are just arbitrary groups of classes intended to help human beings find their way around the class library. Which category a class is in does not affect how it functions *in any way*. It only affects where it appears in the system browser.

In a similar way, the methods inside a class are organised into logical groups called *protocols*. Again, which protocol a method is in does not affect how it functions in any way. Protocols exist solely to partition the methods a class implements in ways which programmers find useful when thinking about the tasks the methods perform.

With this knowledge in mind we can now look at the way the system browser works. The top left pane of the window contains a list of all the categories in the image. When a category has been selected by clicking on it with the mouse, the next pane across will contain a list of all the classes in that particular category. When a class has been selected the next pane will contain a list of all the protocols in that class. When a protocol has been selected the right-most pane will contain a list of all the methods in that protocol. Finally, selecting a method displays its source-code in the large lower pane of the system browser window.

You will have noticed that below the list of classes is a pair of radio buttons which are rather confusingly labelled *instance* and *class*. These buttons control whether the browser is looking at *instance* methods or *class* methods. This distinction is sometimes referred to as the 'instance-side' versus the 'class-side'. If you are confused by this distinction try rereading chapter 2, or try thinking of class methods as the instructions which factory objects (classes) understand, and instance methods as the instructions which the objects the factories make (instances) will understand. Remember that even when *instance* is selected, you're not looking at actual *instances* of the class. You're looking at the methods the instances of the class will understand when they are instantiated (created).

Browser Commands

Each of the four top panes of the system browser window pops up a different menu when the *operate* mouse button is used on them. The menus contain commands used to manipulate categories, classes, protocols and methods respectively. We'll look at many of these commands in more detail in Part II.

Each of the menus also allows you to **spawn** (open) another browser which looks at just the code in that particular category, class, protocol, or method. This is a useful facility which you should use when you're particularly interested in a part of the system and don't need a full system browser. In addition, the menu you get in the class pane allows you to **spawn hierarchy**. This opens a browser which *does* organise classes according to their position in the inheritance hierarchy, instead of according to which category they're in. The *hierarchy browser* will show just that part of the tree relevant to the class selected at the time it is opened (that is, all the class's superclasses and subclasses). If you want to see the whole tree, just open a hierarchy browser on the class **Object**.

Creating New Code with a Browser

The various browsers are the fundamental way in which you write and add new code to the Smalltalk system. At the end of this chapter is a worked example of how to do this which you may find useful if you haven't yet written any of your own code.

There is one slight irregularity. If you want to create a new category in the system or a new protocol in a class, you do so by using the **add...** command from the category or protocol menus. However, if you want to create a new class in a category or a new method in a protocol, you do so by filling in the template provided in the bottom pane when the category or protocol is selected (and no class or method is selected respectively). The important menu command here is **accept** which puts what you have typed through the compiler and adds it to the system code (provided there are no errors).

There are lots of other commands in the operate menus of the various browsers (including the **file out as...** command used to save your code to individual files instead of the whole image if you desire).

You should try to explore them as they have all been put in the system by experienced Smalltalk programmers and are all very useful in the right circumstances. Once again, Part II of this book will help you make the best use of these commands.

Inspectors

The various browsers we have just looked at provide a way of examining the Smalltalk classes in your image. *Inspectors* on the other hand, provide a way of looking at Smalltalk *instances*. Although there are actually several kinds of inspector, the system selects whichever is needed to look at the kind of object you're attempting to inspect. Because of this, and the fact that the different inspectors behave almost identically, you can think of them as being the same.

Inspectors are opened by using the **inspect** command available on many *operate* menus to inspect the result of evaluating the selected expression, or by sending the message **inspect** to any object. Every time you open an inspector, you are opening a window on a single object. Once open, you can't change which object the inspector is looking at. If you want to look at another object, open another inspector. Smalltalk programmers will frequently have many inspectors open on the their screens at the same time, especially during debugging!

The inspector window below is divided into two panes. On the left is a list of the instance variables in the object. Selecting one of these will display the current value of the variable in the right-hand part of the window. Each pane of the window has its own *operate* menu. On the left the menu usually just allows you to open another inspector (**inspect**) on the object contained in the selected instance variable. In

A typical inspector, in this case inspecting an instance of class **PopUpMenu**.

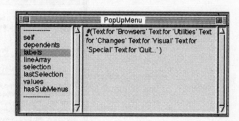

the case of collection objects (see chapter 7) you will also be able to **add** and **remove** objects from the collection. The operate menu for the right-hand pane of the window allows you to do many more things, including execute code (**do it**, **print it**, **inspect**) in the context of the object being inspected. This means you can send messages to the object by typing an expression involving `self` into the right-hand pane (for example, `self initialize`) selecting it, and then evaluating it. You can also use **accept** to put new values into the instance variables.

One thing to note very carefully is that inspectors do not automatically update themselves when an object changes. If you're using an inspector to look at the value of an instance variable in an object, and the value changes (perhaps because a message has been sent to the object from elsewhere), the inspector will continue to display the old value. To see the new value, you should deselect the instance variable, then reselect it. You don't need to open a new inspector to do this, you just need to click twice on the instance variable.

Notifiers and Debuggers

We will be covering debugging in much more detail in Part II—*The Art of Smalltalk*, but since you are unlikely to get as far as that without encountering at least one error, it's worth briefly talking about Smalltalk's notifiers and debuggers (shown below) here.

Notifiers from *VisualWorks* 2.0 (front) and an earlier version of Smalltalk (behind). Both were generated when the system realised that nil doesn't understand the message `wibble`.

```
┌─────────────────────────────────────────────────────┐
│ ▓▓▓▓ Unhandled exception: Message not understood: #wibble ▓▓▓▓ │
├─────────────────────────────────────────────────────┤
│ Unhandled exception: Message not understood: #wibble │
│ UndefinedObject(Object)>>doesNotUnderstand:          │
│ UndefinedObject>>unboundMethod                       │
│ UndefinedObject(Object)>>performMethod:arguments:    │
│ UndefinedObject(Object)>>performMethod:              │
│ Compiler(SmalltalkCompiler)>>evaluate:in:receiver:notifying:ifFail: │
└─────────────────────────────────────────────────────┘
```

```
┌───────────────────────────────────────────────┐
│ ▓▓▓            Exception              ▓▓▓       │
├───────────────────────────────────────────────┤
│  ⊘  Unhandled exception: Message not           │
│     understood: #wibble                        │
│                                                │
│  ┌─────────┐  ┌─────────┐  ┌─────────┐         │
│  │  Debug  │  │ Proceed │  │Terminate│         │
│  └─────────┘  └─────────┘  └─────────┘         │
│     ┌────────────┐  ┌────────────┐             │
│     │ Copy stack │  │ Correct it...│           │
│     └────────────┘  └────────────┘             │
│                                                │
│ UndefinedObject(Object)>>doesNotUnderstand:    │
│ UndefinedObject>>unboundMethod                 │
│ UndefinedObject(Object)>>performMethod:arguments: │
│ UndefinedObject(Object)>>performMethod:        │
│ Compiler(SmalltalkCompil...eiver:notifying:ifFail: │
└───────────────────────────────────────────────┘
```

Whenever the Smalltalk system encounters an error (very often a message it does not understand, but also an overflow, a halt message or any other exceptional situation in which it cannot proceed), it will pop up a small window called a *Notifier*. The notifier contains a stack back-trace which, if you know how to interpret it, will tell you exactly the situation which led up to the error. The notifier also offers you the opportunity to do various things including attempt to proceed, open a debugger window (see below) or simply terminate the execution of your code, returning to the development environement. In earlier versions of Smalltalk, these options were on a pop-up menu, whilst the latest version of *VisualWorks* puts them on push buttons. If when you get a notifier you select **Debug**, you will get a debugger window which is a very powerful tool that's actually a cross between a notifier, a browser and two inspectors.

The next diagram shows a typical debugger window. At the top is a repeat of the stack back-trace leading up to the error. Each line shows a particular message being sent to a particular object. If you select a line you can browse the code involved in the middle pane. Here you can single-step the code (using the **step** button) or 'drill-down' into the messages being sent (using the **send** button). You can also modify the code (by editing it and using **accept** from the pop-up menu), and continue execution.

At the bottom of the debugger are what are in effect two inspectors embedded into the window. The left-hand inspector allows you to see and modify the instance variables of the object selected in the stack back-trace at the top. The right-hand inspector allows you to see and modify the values of the temporary variables defined in, and parameters being sent to, the method being displayed.

A debugger opened after the system has failed to understand the message **start**.

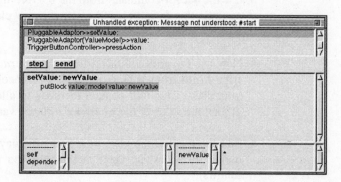

49

Trying Things Out

If you haven't already done so, now is probably a good time to actually sit in front of your Smalltalk system and explore a few of the things we've been talking about so far. It's really up to you to test and enhance your understanding by trying out whatever you like. Here are some simple ideas if you're stuck for somewhere to start though.

First of all, try evaluating some simple message expressions in a workspace window (you can open a workspace from the launcher). For example, you might like to try:

1 + 1.   (select this one with the mouse and use **print it**)
Transcript show: 'Hello!'.   (use **do it** with this one)

You may also like to try defining a simple class with one instance variable and a couple of methods as follows:

1. Open a *system browser* (again, from the launcher) and use the **add** command from the *operate* menu in the category pane (upper-left) to create a new category called for example, **Test Classes**.

2. The browser will now be displaying a class definition template in the code pane (lower half of the window). To define a new class you need to edit this template so that it looks like this:

```
Object subclass: #TestClass
    instanceVariableNames: 'testVar'
    classVariableNames: ''
    poolDictionaries: ''
    category: 'Test Classes'
```

3. Use the **accept** command from the *operate* menu of the code pane to compile this definition and create the new class **TestClass** with a single instance variable called **testVar**.

4. Now use the **add** command from the *operate* menu of the protocol pane (third from left) to add a new protocol called **accessing** to your class. This will contain methods to allow other objects to get and set the value of the **testVar** instance variable.

5. Edit the method template now being displayed in the code view to define an accessing (get) method for the *variable* **testVar** as follows:

```
testVar
    ^testVar.
```

6. Use the **accept** command from the *operate* menu of the code pane to compile this method definition and so create a new *method* called **testVar**.

7. Delete the previous code from the code pane and replace it with the code for an accessing (set) method for the variable **testVar** as follows:

```
testVar: anObject
    testVar := anObject.
```

8. Add this method to the class using the **accept** command as before.

Having defined a new class with a couple of methods in a browser, you can now explore making instances of this class from a workspace, inspecting them, and sending them messages to get and set the value of the instance variable. For example, back in a workspace try:

```
MyInstance := TestClass new.    (Select and inspect)
MyInstance testVar: 'A string'. (Select and do it)
```

The first time you do this you'll be asked what kind of variable **MyInstance** is to be defined as. Make it a global variable. If you've got an inspector open on an instance of your class and you change the value of its instance variable using the **testVar:** message, remember that you'll need to deselect and reselect the instance variable in the inspector in order to see the change.

Summary

This chapter has introduced the second of the three parts of the Smalltalk world—the Smalltalk development environment. You should now have a basic understanding of the various different programming tools in the *VisualWorks* system. These include the launcher from which everything is controlled, and the transcript window where important messages are printed. There are also workspaces for typing message expressions that you want to execute immediately, and browsers for exploring and writing code that you want to add to the system. Classes, their variables and methods are defined using the browser tools. There are inspectors for looking at object instances, and finally there are the notifiers which pop up when errors occur, and the debuggers used to find and fix problems.

With luck you will now feel confident enough about using these tools to enter and evaluate simple Smalltalk expressions. You may also have been able to define your own classes and tried making a few instances of them. Most importantly, you should know how to use the system browser to view the system class hierarchy, because that is the subject of the next chapter.

Chapter 6

The Smalltalk Class Library

Having described the Smalltalk language, and briefly introduced the Smalltalk development environment, we can now complete the picture by looking at the Smalltalk *class library*. There are over 1300 classes in the standard *VisualWorks* image—many more than this if you have filed in any optional extras, or are trying to use someone else's classes. When writing Smalltalk programs you cannot avoid reusing these classes, and in many ways the more you can reuse, the better. However, to document all of the classes in detail would require thousands of pages. Fortunately this is not necessary.

A good proportion of the classes in the class library are there to make the system work (because 'Smalltalk is written in Smalltalk'), and are not intended to be reused directly by you. Despite this, it can still be interesting to have a passing knowledge of these classes, as long as you remember that you don't *have* to understand all the complexity you are exposed to!

Out of the remainder of the classes there are a few you will use all the time and will come to have a good knowledge of simply because you use them almost without thinking (objects like strings, booleans, collections and other common objects fall into this category).

In general though you will find that you know very little about most of the classes in the system until you actually need to use them. At that time being able to make good use of the browser tools and having a good idea of the general features you are looking for will mean that you are able to find the kind of functionality you are looking for without having to go to the manual.

The purpose of this chapter then is to give you a *road-map* for the Smalltalk class library, and to teach you a little about map reading. We're going to take a tour of the class library, stopping every so often to look at important classes which you might like to come back to later. You'll also find that the class library contains many examples of good Smalltalk 'style'. Later chapters describe some of these classes in more detail. First though, we need to take a look at the common things we'll see on the way.

The Standard Protocols

In the previous chapter we mentioned that the Smalltalk development environment separates the methods in each class into groups called *protocols*. These are not random partitions, but are intended to reflect the purpose which the methods serve. Remember that this grouping is intended to help *programmers*, and does not affect the functioning of the system in any way.

The programmers who are helped by the existence of protocols fall into two camps. There are the original writers of the classes—and of course for your classes you'll be in this camp. However, there are also the *reusers* of the classes. For the classes in the standard Smalltalk library you'll fall into this second camp. This means that the names of the protocols form a vital clue to the purpose and functionality of the methods inside.

Although they perform different functions, many Smalltalk classes have methods which are conceptually similar. Over the years, Smalltalk programmers have evolved a set of names for the protocols which contain these methods. By understanding these protocols (and adhering to the conventions when you write your own classes), you will be able to understand the functioning of a particular class much more easily.

Before we tour around the class library, we're going to take a look at just some of the standard protocols. These are the most common ones, and they illustrate how the name of the protocol relates to the types of method inside.

initialize-release

This protocol contains methods to do with initialising new instances of the class, and (less frequently) releasing them (tidying up at the end of their lifetimes). The usual name for a method which initialises an object is **initialize**, and the usual name for a method which tidies up afterwards is **release**.

accessing

This important protocol contains methods which provide access to the normally private instance variables of an object. If you followed the example class definition at the end of the last chapter you will have already created methods of this kind.

There are two types of **accessing** method. There are the 'get' methods, which return the value of an instance variable, and the 'set' methods ,which allow you to set the value of an instance variable to a particular object. By convention, 'get' methods are simply named exactly the same as the instance variable they return, whilst 'set' methods have the same name with a trailing colon (:) and of course take a single parameter. You can infer from the existence (or otherwise) of 'get' and 'set' methods in a class whether the writer of the classes intended you to have access to the instance variables of instances of that class.

testing

The **testing** protocol contains methods which will typically return either **true** or **false** when asked about some characteristic of the object (for example, **isEven** asked of an **integer**, or **isNil** asked of any object).

comparing

The **comparing** protocol contains similar methods to **testing**, except that they take a parameter against which to compare the object before returning **true** or **false**. For example, you could imagine an expression like **colour1 isMoreBlueThan: colour2** which might return **true** or **false**. The method **isMoreBlueThan:** would rightfully belong in a protocol called **comparing**.

displaying

This protocol applies in particular to the classes which implement the Smalltalk graphical user interface. It contains the methods which actually draw objects on the screen, especially the important method, **displayOn:**. Most classes which have anything to do with displaying things on the screen will have this protocol. This is the place to go first if you want to alter or just understand the way things look.

printing

Many of the fundamental classes have a **printing** protocol. It contains methods which can produce a representation of the object in printed form. We'll see very shortly how every object in the system has this capability.

updating

This protocol always contains a special set of methods to do with receiving notifications about changes in other objects. These methods are described in Chapter 8—*The Dependency Mechanism*.

private

The **private** protocol contains methods whose usage the writer of the class wishes to restrict. This is not enforced by the system, but is a matter of convention. Often, private methods are not intended to be used outside the class in which they are defined. That is, they're only intended to be called by other methods in the same class. Sometimes subclasses will also use them, and occasionally they will be used amongst groups of tightly coupled classes. Whatever the intention, although you *can* use **private** methods, be very aware that you're being warned that they are considered private and are especially likely to change between releases of the system. You have been warned!

instance-creation

This is a protocol you will find in some classes on the 'class-side' (by pressing the *class* button in the browser). This protocol contains methods which the *class* understands, and which make and return new instances of the class. Usually these methods will be specialised in some way appropriate to the particular class. So, if you find a class you want to use, this is the place to go to find out how to make an instance of it. However, if the class doesn't have an **instance-creation** protocol, that doesn't necessarily mean you can't make instances. It's probable that the class just uses the methods it inherits from its superclass. By opening a class hierarchy browser you'll be able to look up the tree to find a class which has an **instance-creation** protocol.

...rary

...ly to start our tour of the Smalltalk class hierarchy. The
...y is in effect a tree of classes branching out from
...e ultimate superclass, **Object** . However, rather than look
...brary by following the hierarchy tree, we'll take advantage
... the development environment groups the classes into
...and tour them in the order they're displayed in the system

...ou want to, you can follow along during or after the tour by
...system browser to look at the classes whilst we're discussing
...Make liberal use of the **hierarchy**, **definition** and **comment**
...ands in the pop-up menu under the class pane (second from left)
... system browser to help your understanding of the purpose of the
...es and how they relate to each other. If you find something else
...interests you, just follow your nose.

Where the classes we come across are important or frequently
used, we'll describe them in detail. Where they're not so frequently
used we'll just mention that they're there. You can browse them for
yourself later or read the manual if you especially need to use these
classes at some stage. Let's go...

Magnitude–General

This first category contains classes to do with representing things which
have 'magnitude'. The root class for this piece of the hierarchy is
Magnitude which simply defines ways of comparing things (**<**, **>=**,
etc.). **Magnitude** in turn inherits from **Object** . Notice how some of
the comparisons are defined in terms of the others. Also, look at how
this class *defines* some of the methods but leaves them to be
implemented lower down in the class hierarchy when the actual way
they must work is known. This deferring of the actual implementation
of a method is typically declared using the message expression **self
subclassResponsibility**. Note that the classes to do with
representing the notions of date and time are also defined in this
category.

Magnitude–Numbers

Here things start to get a little more specific. **Magnitude–Numbers**
contains all the classes the system uses to represent numbers. By
looking here you can discover the different forms in which Smalltalk

can deal with numbers, and look at all the many operations you can perform on number objects.

ArithmeticValue is the abstract (no instances) superclass of this bit of the hierarchy. It contains all the basic operations which all numbers can perform. Subclasses of this class (especially **Number**) add in operations which are appropriate for their particular kind of number. Notice how arithmetic (**+, -, *, /**, ...) which you might have thought of as part of the Smalltalk language, is actually defined here as part of the class hierarchy. There are also mathematical functions, and rounding operations. Finally, there is a method in **Integer** called **timesRepeat:** which when sent to an integer will repeat the block sent as a parameter the appropriate number of times. For example:

```
3 timesRepeat: [Transcript show: 'Hello!'; space].
```

Although this may seem like an important feature of Smalltalk, the power of the other control structures (especially something we'll look at in the next chapter—collection enumeration) means that it is rarely used in practice.

Collections-Abstract

This category and all the subsequent **Collections-** categories contain the *collection* classes. Instances of these classes hold collections of other objects. These are such important and highly reused classes that an entire chapter of this book (Chapter 7—*The Collection Classes*) is devoted to describing them. We'll defer a discussion of them until then.

Graphics-Geometry

Graphics-Geometry contains all the classes whose job it is to represent geometric entities. Especially important are **Point** and **Rectangle**. Instances of **Point** (which is actually a subclass of **ArithmeticValue**, proving how categories are used to describe function not inheritance), represent the notion of a point in a two-dimensional co-ordinate space. As such, they are of vital importance to all the classes which implement the user-interface. Instances of **Rectangle** represent rectangular regions (actually by holding two points), and are equally vital to the user-interface classes.

The rest of the **Graphics-** categories contain classes which represent all the graphical notions the system has to deal with. These include fonts, colours, palettes, images, text and so on. Notice that most of the actual GUI classes (windows, widgets, etc.) are not in these categories, but come later.

Kernel-Objects

We're now reaching the real heart of the class library. **Kernel-Objects** contains probably the most important class in the entire system—**Object**. This class is the root of the Smalltalk class hierarchy, and provides such a wealth of facilities that we will briefly stop our tour here and look at it in more detail.

Object—The Root of the Hierarchy

As we've already observed, every single class in the system ultimately inherits from **Object**. This means that every single object in the system (instances *and* classes) will understand and respond to the messages (or *protocol*) defined in **Object**. Here are some of the things it can do, discussed in the order in which you'll find them in the various protocols of **Object**:

In the **initialize-release** protocol, the **release** method releases all the dependents (see Chapter 8—*The Dependency Mechanism*) that an object might have before it is destroyed. Notice that there is no **initialize** method defined in **Object**. This means that if you send **initialize** to an object which does not define this method somewhere else in its class hierarchy, you will get an error.

In **accessing** there are many methods which provide the foundations for subclasses which store data as collections. The only method in this protocol that you might want to use directly is **yourself**. This method, which just returns **self**, might at first seem rather pointless. However, there are certain rare circumstances in which it is useful. Browse the senders of **yourself** (using the **senders** command in a browser) to see some examples.

In **testing**, the class **Object** defines a whole load of things which its instances are not (**nil**, **integer**, **string** and so on). This is so that these messages can be over-ridden in the appropriate subclasses to return **true** instead of **false**.

In **comparing** we can see the definitions of two very important comparisons in Smalltalk: = and ==. It is *crucial* to understand the difference between these two comparisons. The operator = tests whether two objects are 'equal'. This depends on the class of the object, and if you browse the implementors of = you will find that lots of classes redefine it in appropriate ways (for example, two **Rectangle** instances might be = if their coordinates are the same).

The operator **==** on the other hand, tests whether the receiver of the message and the parameter are 'equivalent'. This means whether they are two references to *the same object*. For example, the expression **rect1 == rect2** would only return **true** if **rect1** and **rect2** were two variables containing the *same* **Rectangle** instance, and not just if they contained two rectangles with the same coordinates. This is a much stronger test than **=**.

The **comparing** protocol also contains methods for hash-coding the object. These are used to provide efficient look up of objects when they are stored in certain kinds of collection.

The **copying** protocol contains methods for producing copies of objects. Smalltalk used to distinguish between a **deepCopy** (the object and all its instance variables were copied recursively), and a **shallowCopy** (the object was copied, but all the copy's instance variables pointed to the same objects as the original). However, **deepCopy** was found to be a fundamentally flawed concept, so now only **shallowCopy** is supported.

The **converting** protocol includes two methods (**->** and **asValue**) for making other objects which contain the receiver as one of their instance variables. These just happen to be so frequently needed that they are included here for convenience.

The protocols **dependents access**, **updating**, **changing** and **dependents collection** are the protocols which contain the methods used to implement the dependency mechanism we'll look at in chapter 8. These methods are described in detail there.

The protocol **printing** contains methods which enable every object in the system to have the printed representation we mentioned earlier. You may have noticed that when you print an object using the development environment, it always describes itself in some useful way (for example **aPopUpMenu**) instead of giving you a useless internal pointer (like **7af41d25**). The method responsible for this is called **printOn:** and it is called whenever the system needs the printed representation of an object. The default definition in **Object** simply uses the name of the object's class, prefixed with '**a**' or '**an**'. Many subclasses of **Object** redefine **printOn:** to generate much more useful strings which actually describe the individual object (for example a **Point** with x-coordinate 3 and y-coordinate 4 would print as **3@4**, instead of just **aPoint**). If you want your objects to print more descriptively, you can also redefine **printOn:** in your class. Look at any of the other implementors of it to see examples.

The **printing** protocol also contains the method **storeString**. This method generates a sequence of characters which form a piece of Smalltalk code. When executed this code will create an object exactly like the object to which the **storeString** message was sent. This remarkable facility is the basis of representing objects in serial form.

The next protocol, **class membership**, provides a set of facilities for testing which class an object is an instance of. Notice especially the difference between **isMemberOf:** (is an instance of a particular class) and **isKindOf:** (is an instance of a particular class *or one of its subclasses*).

The **message handling** protocol contains some important methods of which **perform:** is the simplest. We'll be looking at these methods in chapter 10—*Pluggability and Adaptors*.

The protocol **error handling** includes some useful methods like **halt**. When evaluated this stops execution of the current method and opens a notifier window. This means you can insert breakpoints in your code for debugging reasons simply by putting in the expression **self halt**. The protocol also includes **doesNotUnderstand:**. This message is sent to an object which does not understand a message it is supposed to be executing. Normally, it opens a notifier window, but you can over-ride it to do clever things if you wish.

Finally in this protocol, **shouldNotImplement** and **subclassResponsibility** are messages you can use to indicate that a subclass wants to 'undefine' a method defined in a superclass (preventing it being sent by raising an error if it is), or indicate that a subclass must implement a method which is defined in a superclass.

The **user interface** protocol provides methods that allow you to **inspect** any object, or **browse** its class. Just sending **inspect** or **browse** to any object will open the appropriate tool.

The remaining protocols in **Object** contain methods which are used internally and are unlikely to be of direct use to programmers. However, feel free to browse them if you want to understand more about how the system works.

A Tour of the Class Library (continued)

Having stopped off to consider the most important class of all—**Object**—in more detail, we can now continue our tour of the Smalltalk class library where we left off.

Kernel-Objects

Besides **Object**, this category also contains some other very commonly used classes which are essential to the functioning of the system. In particular, the classes **Boolean**, **True** and **False** implement all of the functionality to do with logical operations in Smalltalk. The class **Boolean** defines all the operations, but they are actually implemented in its subclasses—**True** and **False**. Each of these subclasses has a single instance called **true** and **false** respectively. Browsing **Boolean** will show you all the kinds of logical operations (**&**, **|**, **not**, etc.) which Smalltalk supports, and the kinds of control structure (**ifFalse:**, **ifTrue:**, etc.) you can use.

Notice how once again, things you might have thought would be part of the *language* (like arithmetic) are actually a part of the class library. For example, a conditional statement is implemented by sending the message **ifTrue:** to an object with a block as the parameter. The block is executed only if the object was an instance of class **True**, and not if it was an instance of class **False**. For example:

```
27 > (3+4) ifTrue: [Transcript show: 'Bigger!'].
```

Browse the implementation of **ifTrue:** in the classes **True** and **False** to see how this works. Do note though, that although this particular functionality is expressed as a set of methods, the compiler can actually spot these messages being sent and compile them 'in-line', optimising their execution. This means that changing the definitions of **ifTrue:** or **ifFalse:** (dangerous as that might otherwise be) won't actually have the effect you might intend. It also means that the debugger will sometimes get confused about where exactly any errors in the use of these messages are located in your source-code.

Look carefully at the difference between **&** and **and:** (also **|** and **or:**) in the boolean classes. The first pair of methods (**&** and **|**) take an expression as their argument, and are *guaranteed* to execute that expression. The second pair of methods (**and :** and **or :**) take a block as their argument, and will *only* execute that block if its value is needed to resolve the logical value of the whole expression. This means that if the expression or block used as an argument has a side-effect as well as returning a value, the choice of **&** or **and:** (**|** or **or:**) is critical. For example, in the first of the following two expressions **fred** will be set to **true**. In the second it won't because there's no need to evaluate the block to know that the whole expression is **true**.

```
(1=1) | (fred := true).
(1=1) or: [fred := true].
```

Another important class in this category is **UndefinedObject**. The system contains only a single instance of this class, called **nil**. Many of the methods **UndefinedObject** implements are to do with undoing the functionality inherited from **Object**! The value **nil** is used to represent the notion of 'nothing' or 'undefined'. It is also the value to which all newly declared variables are initialised.

Finally in the **Kernel-Objects** category, the class **Model** is simply a subclass of **Object** which implements dependency (see chapter 8 again) differently for efficiency reasons.

Kernel-Classes

This category contains all the classes which implement the very notion of a 'class' in Smalltalk. This really is the internals of the system, and can be very confusing. However it is useful to know that just as all *objects* can understand the messages defined in the class **Object**, all *classes* can understand the messages defined in the classes **Behavior**, **ClassDescription** and **Class** (which inherit from each other in that order). This is because class objects are *instances* of the class **Class** (think about it, but don't worry if you find it confusing).

There is some very useful functionality in **Behavior**, especially for accessing the subclasses and superclasses of a class, and finding all its instances (**allInstances**). The latter message can be very useful during debugging, but remember you can only send it to a *class*.

Perhaps the most important single message defined in the **Kernel-Classes** category is **new**. This is the message you can send to any class to ask it to make and return a new instance of itself. You might think that this should be defined on the class side of **Object**, but in fact because of the complexities of the Smalltalk class system (which we shall *not* be going into here), it is defined on the instance side of **Behavior**. This still means that any and every class understands the message **new**, although many provide more appropriate instance creation methods too. Note though that some classes which are intended never to have instances (abstract superclasses) explicitly 'un-implement' the **new** method. They do this by over-riding it with the expression **self shouldNotImplement**.

The rest of the **Kernel** categories deal with internal things which again are probably not of much immediate interest. The only exceptions are the class **Process**, which implements and provides access to Smalltalk's own lightweight process mechanism (look in the manual for more details), and the class **BlockClosure**, which implements the block notion we looked at in the previous chapter.

BlockClosure also provides some more of the Smalltalk control structures which are sprinkled around the class hierarchy. In particular there are the methods **repeat**, **whileFalse**, **whileTrue**, and their variants. You can browse their implementations to see how they work but here is an example:

```
[MyWindow isTooBig] whileFalse: [MyWindow grow].
```

Interface-Framework

This and the remainder of the **Interface-** categories contain all the classes which implement the Smalltalk user-interface. These categories, together with all the **UIBasics** and **UILooks** categories, contain hundreds of different classes for implementing widgets, windows and everything in between. Thankfully, because of the existence of the *VisualWorks* GUI building tools (implemented by classes in the **UIPainter** and **UIBuilder** categories) you will rarely need to access all these classes explicitly. Remember though that if you need to do so, (and if you want to build user-interfaces which *VisualWorks* doesn't support, you will) the source-code is here for you to browse, understand and use. A few of these classes are important enough, and illustrate such useful general principles, that we will be describing them in more detail in Chapter 10—*Pluggability and Adaptors*.

Tools-Programming

This and the rest of the **Tools-** categories contain the classes which implement the browsers, inspectors, debuggers and so on that we looked at in chapter 5. If you don't like the way any of these tools behave, this is the place to go to find out how they work, and modify them.

System-Changes

This and the other **System-** categories contain the classes used by the Smalltalk compiler. Unless you really want to modify the internals of the system, you should never have any need to go near these classes.

OS-Window System

This category contains classes used to interface Smalltalk to the underlying window system. This is the place to go if you are interested in gaining access to that mechanism for any reason. However, for normal GUI programming you should have no need to deal with any of these classes. The only exception is perhaps the class `Cursor`. This class provides methods you can use if you want to change the shape of the mouse cursor.

OS-Streaming

The classes in here provide support for accessing files in the underlying operating system. Sometimes you may want to create instances of these classes directly, but more usually you would use an instance of the class `Filename` to create one for you.

OS-Support

This category contains the class `Filename`, which is your easiest and most portable route to opening a file in the underlying filesystem.

OS-Unix, OS-Dos, OS-Mac

These categories contain classes which specialise the abstract notions of filename and other things which Smalltalk deals with, to the particular platform which the virtual machine is actually running on. They enable some of the cross-platform portability which *VisualWorks* provides.

External-Collections

This and the other `External-` categories contain classes which represent entities to do with connecting Smalltalk up to other languages such as C or C++. How you do this depends to a large extent on exactly what sort of machine you have, so you'll need to look in the manual for details.

UIExamples

Finally in this tour of the class library, the various `UIExamples` categories contain the many classes used to implement the example applications provided as part of the *VisualWorks* system. This is a good place to start if you want to try modifying some of these examples applications, or need to find out how they implement a particular piece of behaviour.

Summary

We've now completed our introduction to the Smalltalk class library. If you've followed the tour, you should find that you're familiar (both from the descriptions given here, and from just browsing around) with some of the standard *protocols* which exist in many of the system classes. You should also have an idea how to predict from the name of a protocol the kinds of method it will contain.

You should now know something about the messages all objects understand (defined in class **Object**), and the messages all classes understand (defined in **Behavior**, **ClassDescription** and **Class**).

You should know where to find arithmetic operations defined (**ArithmeticValue** and its subclasses) and where to find logical operations and control structures (**Boolean** and its subclasses). Finally, you should have a good idea of what kinds of functionality the rest of the class library contains.

The remainder of this part of the book is concerned with more detailed descriptions of some of the features and classes we've mentioned here. The classes have been chosen not only because they are useful to know about, but also because they illustrate some of the style of good Smalltalk programming. Part II of the book then goes on to explain how you can learn even more about the Smalltalk system for yourself, and more importantly how you can design your own classes to fit in with it.

The Collection Classes

Now that we have a general road-map of the Smalltalk class library, we can start to look at some of the classes in more detail. The first set of classes we will consider are the collection classes. The various types of collection are some of the most highly reused and reusable classes in the system. In fact, every Smalltalk programmer uses them in almost every program. The classes themselves are highly developed (although they are not necessarily the most *efficient* implementation), and provide a good example of Smalltalk programming style.

They're also an example of something else we'll be returning to again and again. A book of this size can't hope to present a complete description of every feature and facility in every type of object. Even the Smalltalk manual doesn't do that, and even if it could it wouldn't necessarily be up to date. No, the only place to go if you want to know *for sure* if a particular feature exists, how it works or how it's implemented, is the system itself. For now, you should concentrate on understanding the basic concepts of the collection classes. Later, you'll be able to use the class hierarchy browser (or any other browser) to explore the different collection classes, consider the alternatives and find out what you really need to know for your specific problem.

What is a Collection?

A collection is an object which *contains* a group of other objects. The contained objects are known as the *elements* of the collection. The diagram over the page shows the idea. No matter what programming language you've used before, you're probably familiar with at least one type of collection—the array. Arrays are available in Smalltalk but

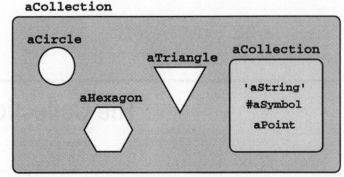

A collection containing objects of various kinds, including another collection object.

there are also various other collection classes provided in the class library. Each one is specialised in various ways, but they all have certain features in common. For example, they all allow you to *add* and *remove* objects from the collection. They also all allow you to *test* the collection and its contents in various ways. Most importantly though, they all allow you to *enumerate* the collection—performing the same operation on each and every element.

Almost all collections in Smalltalk are *heterogeneous*. That is, they can contain a mixture of any kinds of object. Remember that Smalltalk is typeless. This means that unlike other languages you don't have to ask the system for 'an array of type integer' for example. You just ask for an array. Importantly, this means that collections can, and frequently do, contain other collections as well.

The exceptions to this heterogeneity rule are classes like **String** and **Symbol** (yes, they're implemented as collections) which can only contain characters, and **ByteArray** which as its name suggests, contains only bytes.

The various collection classes form quite a complex inheritance hierarchy under the root class, **Collection**. All the basic functionality of every collection is defined in the **Collection** class, and it's probably a good idea to browse through it using one of the system's code browsers, just to become familiar with the kinds of things all types of collection can do.

Below **Collection**, there are a number of *abstract superclasses* in the hierarchy. Like **Collection** itself, no instances of these classes ever exist. They serve just to group together functionality. Don't try making instances of these classes—they won't work properly. You can tell if a class is abstract or concrete by looking at its class comment using a browser.

Remember that sometimes, when you're looking for a particular feature in a particular kind of collection, it won't be in the particular collection subclass, and it won't be in **Collection**. It'll be hiding in the middle, in one of these abstract superclasses.

Towards the bottom of the hierarchy are the *concrete classes*. Depending on the version of Smalltalk you're using, there may be over fifty concrete subclasses of **Collection** in as many as eight different system categories. Many of these have very specialised uses in the system. However, when *you* need a collection in your program, you should normally be able to choose from one of these concrete classes: **Array**; **Bag**; **Dictionary**; **OrderedCollection**; **Set**; **SortedCollection**; and **Interval**. In the rest of this chapter we'll concern ourselves with just these classes.

Creating Collection Instances

Here are four ways of making new collection instances. You can try them out individually using a workspace and **inspect** :

```
MyColl := OrderedCollection new.
MyColl := Array new: 27.
MyColl := Set with: #red with: #green with: #blue.
MyColl := #('Goodbye'  4  #now).
```

The first way of making a collection is the most basic, and simply makes an empty ordered collection. All collection classes, like all other classes, know how to do this. The second way makes a new array, with twenty-seven elements. The third way will make a set containing the three symbols **#red**, **#green** and **#blue**. Note that **with:with:with:** is a single method with three parameters. Also provided are the methods **with:**, **with:with:** and **with:with:with:with:**. After four elements you're expected to make the collection and then add the elements in one by one using **add:**. Finally, the fourth way is a useful shorthand used to create arrays. This example makes an array with three elements (**'Goodbye'**, **4** and **#now**). This only works if the elements are *literals*. In other words, you cannot put pieces of Smalltalk code inside the parentheses. This is a common mistake and can lead to some bizarre results. This is because the expression is put through the compiler, creating the array at compile-time. It is not actually evaluated (executed) at run-time.

Choosing Which Collection to Use

When you want to use a collection in a Smalltalk program, it can help to ask these questions:

1. Do the elements of the collection need to be *ordered*?
2. If yes, how will the ordering be *determined*?
3. Will the elements be accessed via a *key*?
4. Will *duplicate* elements be allowed in the collection?

Your answers to these questions will help determine what type of collection you need. There are a couple of important things to keep in mind though. First, as often happens in programming, especially in Smalltalk, there is no one right answer. If a particular collection class seems to do the job, use it, at least until you have a reason not to. Choosing a collection class depends on style as much as need. Second, you very rarely need to create new subclasses of **Collection**. The various subclasses provided in the class hierarchy should almost always include what you need. Usually when you want to add functionality to a collection you should *encapsulate* a collection in an instance of one of your own classes, and add the functionality there. This business of encapsulation as an alternative to inheritance is important enough that we'll be returning to it in Part II.

The Different Kinds of Collection

Having discussed the basic characteristics of the collection classes, let's take a look in a little more detail at the specific classes you might consider using in your code.

Array

These are very like the arrays provided in other languages. Elements are inserted and retrieved using an integer index (or in the terms used above, an integer *key*). To retrieve an element use the **at:** method. To add an element use the **at:put:** method. For example the code:

```
MyArray := Array new: 20.
MyArray at: 12 put: #yellow.
MyArray at: 17.
```

creates an empty twenty element array, assigning it to the variable **MyArray**. It then puts the symbol **#yellow** in position **12** of

MyArray, and finally returns the **17**th element of **MyArray** (which in this case would be **nil**). *Note that in Smalltalk, unlike some other languages, arrays start at* 1 *not at* 0!

Bag

A **Bag** is simply an unordered, unkeyed, collection of objects. You put objects in using **add:**, and remove them using **remove:**. For example:

```
MyBag add: MyNewColour.
MyBag remove: MyOldColour.
```

Like other kinds of collection **B ag** also understands **addAll:** and **removeAll:** which, when used with a collection as the argument will add or remove all the elements in that collection from the bag.

It might seem peculiar to have a kind of collection in which you cannot retrieve an object unless you've already got it. However, bags are useful when you want to test *whether* a collection contains an object, or iterate over a collection of objects. We'll look at both of these features of collections shortly.

Note that the same object can be in a bag *more than once*. In this case **Bag** keeps a tally of how many times an object is in it. Note also that Bag uses **=** to test whether an object is in itself before incrementing its tally. This means that if you try to add in an object which is equal to one already in the **Bag**, but not equivalent to it (that is, not the same object), it won't get added—the tally for the equal object will be incremented instead. Again, if this doesn't make sense don't worry. Just remember to think about it if you start getting unexpected behaviour when using a **Bag**!

Dictionary

Dictionary is one of the most useful collection classes—when you know how to use it. You can think of dictionaries as being like arrays, except that instead of using integers for the indexes or keys of the collection, you can use *any object at all*. For example:

```
MyDictionary at: #name put: 'Simon'.
MyDictionary at: #age.
```

puts the string **'Simon'** into **MyDictionary**, giving it the key **#name**, and then retrieves the object previously put into the dictionary with the key **#age**. The string **'Simon'** and whatever object had the key **#age**, are called *values*. In this way, a dictionary keeps a mapping between

A **Dictionary** holding a
mapping between objects called
keys and other objects called
values.

Keys	Values
'Britain'	'Pounds'
'France'	'Francs'
'USA'	'Dollars'

one set of objects (the keys) and another set of objects (the values). It is
quite common to use symbols as keys in a dictionary. However, the
keys and values in the dictionary really can be any kind of object. This
is a powerful facility which you'll probably find increasingly useful.

The diagram above shows an example of a simple dictionary
which maps the names of countries to the names of their currencies (all
held as strings). The following code would create a dictionary like the
one in the diagram:

```
MyDictionary := Dictionary new.
MyDictionary at: 'Britain' put: 'Pounds';
             at: 'France' put: 'Francs';
             at: 'USA' put: 'Dollars'.
```

OrderedCollection

This is the class most frequently used instead of **Array** when a
collection of objects must be kept and accessed in a particular order.
Unlike arrays though, that order is determined by each element's
position relative to another, rather than by an integer index.

Instances of **OrderedCollection** grow and shrink as elements
are added and removed. Methods like **add:**, **addFirst:**, **addLast:**,
add:before:, **add:after:** and others provide a lot of flexibility for
inserting new elements into the collection. Elements may be retrieved
with **first** and **last**, and removed with the methods **removeFirst**,
removeLast, and **remove:**. These methods allow an instance of
OrderedCollection to be used as if it were a queue or a stack. Note
that if you use **remove:** to try to remove an element from a collection
it isn't actually in, you will get an error. Another method,
remove:ifAbsent: allows you to specify what should happen if the
element wasn't in the collection:

```
MyCollection remove: MyName ifAbsent: [].
```

This is a useful construction which quietly does nothing if **MyName** wasn't in **MyCollection**. The **[]** is an empty block which simply returns when it is run.

Whenever in another language you would think 'I need an array', you should in Smalltalk be thinking 'Would an **OrderedCollection** be better'? Unless you explicitly know the size of the collection, and it's fixed in size, or you need the efficiency which arrays provide (very roughly twice as fast as **OrderedCollection**), you should choose **OrderedCollection**. Don't be trapped into choosing **Array** just because it's more efficient or more familiar. Very often using **OrderedCollection** will give much more elegant and flexible code, which may be just as fast in your application. Give it a try.

Note that although you *can* access the elements of an **OrderedCollection** using **at:** and **at:put:** —that is, by using integer indexes—you should probably avoid doing so unless you're very sure you know the indexes and you've remembered that they'll all change if you send an **addFirst:** message or anything similar to your collection.

Set

This class represents the mathematical notion of a set of objects. Sets are collections in which there are no duplicates. Unlike a **Bag**, or an **OrderedCollection**, it does not matter how many times you try to add an element into a set (using **add:**)—the set will still only contain the element once. This automatic throwing away of duplicates is sometimes useful.

Note that **Set** uses = to decide whether a new element is already in itself and so shouldn't be added. This means that two different objects can't be in the same **Set** if they happen to be equal. If you want a set which rejects new members only when they're equivalent (==) to existing elements rather than just because they're equal (=), use **IdentitySet**. As a side-effect, because == is a faster test than = (which can involve arbitrary amounts of testing of instance variables), **IdentitySet** is usually faster than **Set**.

Elements in a set are not held in any particular order. When you print out a set, or iterate over its elements (see below), you can't control what order the elements are accessed in and you shouldn't rely on it being the same every time.

When you use an inspector to look at a set, be aware that although the set displays itself correctly when you select **self**, it may look as though it contains extra **nil** elements in its instance variables. These are internal to the way **Set** works and can be safely ignored. They won't affect your code because the iteration methods (**do:**, **collect:** and so on) in **Set** know to ignore those elements.

SortedCollection

Instances of this class provide a way in which elements can be collected together in an order determined by some feature of the elements. For example, strings can be sorted alphabetically, or numbers numerically. You don't even have to tell a **SortedCollection** to sort itself. As you add elements in (using **add:**) they are automatically inserted in the right place. **SortedCollection** is not limited to just these types of element or sorting order though. It can sort any objects into an order based on any characteristic, provided you give it the necessary *hooks*. Giving it these hooks does require an understanding of some features of Smalltalk which you may not yet feel comfortable with. Don't worry if you don't understand the following description. **SortedCollections** are not too common—come back to it when you feel comfortable with using blocks of Smalltalk code.

   SortedCollection uses a replaceable piece of Smalltalk code, held in a block, to capture the comparison that's used to decide whether one object should be before or after another in the collection. Note that we're not talking about the sorting *algorithm* here—that's fixed, and embodied in **SortedCollection**. We're talking about the test which determines whether one object is 'less than' another, or whether it's 'earlier in the alphabet', 'bigger', or 'more green'. The piece of code compares two objects and answers **true** if the objects should be in the order presented, or **false** if they need to be reversed.

   You give an instance of **SortedCollection** one of these pieces of comparison code by sending it with the message **sortBlock:**. Luckily **SortedCollection** provides a default sort block, so in most cases you don't need to worry about it. The default sort block tests whether each element is 'less than' the other elements. This means that any kind of object which understands the **<=** message can be sorted by a default **SortedCollection**. If your objects don't understand the **<=** message you have a choice of writing this method in your class, or providing a sort block which uses a different method. For example, the following block would tell a sorted collection to sort its elements according to the length of their names by doing the appropriate comparison and answering **true** or **false**:

```
[:x :y | x name size < y name size].
```

Interval

This class is slightly different from the other subclasses of `Collection` we've looked at in that it can't hold a collection of arbitrary objects. Instead it actually represents the idea of a 'finite arithmetic progression'. In other words, it *behaves* as if it were a collection of numbers. Instances of class `Interval` are created in a different way from other collections as well. For example, the following two expressions:

```
MyInterval := Interval from: 50 to: 100 by: 2.
MyInterval := 50 to: 100 by: 2.
```

would create an instance of `Interval` which would behave as if it contained the numbers **50, 52, 54,...**, **100**. Notice how in the second case the object **50** provides a 'convenience' method (`to:by:`) which knows how to create an instance of `Interval`. You can find this method and others like it by browsing the class `Number`.

You cannot add new elements to instances of `Interval`. In fact if you look at the definitions of `add:`, `at:put:` and others, you will see that they are explicitly 'un-inherited' from `Collection`. This is an important feature of inheritance in Smalltalk and we'll be returning to it later. The point of this class is that like all collections, it provides a way of iterating over its contents (we'll see how very shortly). In other words, it provides a control structure similar to a do-loop. However, as we've observed before, it's rare that you actually need to construct a loop like this in good Smalltalk code.

Testing Collections

As well as being able to insert, retrieve and remove elements from collections, you can also probe them in various ways to test different characteristics. Each different collection subclass has particular tests, but they all understand the following messages :

size — how many elements the collection contains.
isEmpty — true if the collection is empty.
includes:anObject — true if the collection contains **anObject**.

When you send the message size to a collection, it tells you how many elements are directly contained by the collection, not how many might be contained in other collections contained in the first collection (in other words, it's not *recursive*). You have to work that out for yourself.

Converting Collections

A collection of one type can be converted into a collection of another type by sending it one of the messages **asArray**, **asBag**, **asOrderedCollection**, **asSet**, or **asSortedCollection**. For example if **MyCollection** is an **Array**, the following code fragment will convert it to a **Set** :

    MySet := MyCollection asSet.

Although we talk about *converting* collections, the original collection object is actually not altered, nor is it destroyed. Instead, sending one of the conversion messages to a collection makes a new collection of the new type, and puts the old collection's elements into the new collection as well. The elements themselves are not *copied*. Each individual element is contained in both the old and new collections. Watch out for this if you alter an element—it is a common source of bugs. For example in the diagram below, altering the object **A** in **aSet** will alter the object **A** in **anArray** because it is the same object.

There are a couple of other caveats associated with converting collections. First, when you convert an unordered collection to a collection which has an order, the order will be unpredictable and not necessarily repeatable. Second, the situation with dictionaries is more complicated because they contain both keys and values. By default, the new collection will contain just the values. Send the message **keys** to a dictionary first to get a new collection with just the keys instead. For example:

    MyValues := MyDictionary asSet.
    MyKeys := MyDictionary keys asSortedCollection.

Sending **aSet** the message **asArray** creates a new collection containing the same elements : A, B, C and D.

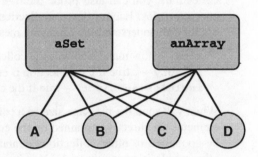

Enumerating Collections

All subclasses of **Collection** understand a set of messages called enumerators. These are all to do with performing the same operation on every element of the collection. However, different enumerators have different specific effects.

The enumerators are one of the most powerful and convenient facilities of collections. Knowing how to use them will make writing some pieces of code simpler than you ever imagined possible. In fact, it is these methods which mean that constructions such as 'do-loops' are so rare in Smalltalk code.

We'll summarise the six different types of enumerator here and then explain them in more detail below:

do: — does the same operation on every element of the collection.

collect: — like **do:** but returns a collection of the results.

select: — tests every element and returns those which pass.

reject: — tests every element and returns those which fail.

detect: — returns the first element which passes the test.

inject:into: — feeds the result of one operation into the next.

do:

The most basic of all the enumerators is **do:** . It simply repeats the same operation for every element in a collection. For example, the expression:

```
MyCollection do: [:piece | piece reset].
```

sends the message **reset** to every element in **MyCollection** . For the purpose of this example we neither know nor care what **reset** does. The code inside the square brackets is a block of Smalltalk which gets executed once for each element in **MyCollection**. The word **:piece** before the vertical bar |, simply says that we'll be using the name **piece** to refer to each element in turn in the code after the | . Every time the block is executed the next element of the collection is substituted for **piece** in the expression **piece reset** .

You can see that the **do:** message allows us to iterate through **MyCollection** very simply, without knowing how big it is, without having to set up our own loop, and without having to increment and test a counter as we might in other languages. However, if you really want to set up a control structure similar to a do-loop in other languages, you

could send the same **do:** message to an instance of the class
Interval. Try this:

```
(10 to: 35 by: 5) do:
        [:i | Transcript show: i printString; cr].
```

You can use **do:** with any kind of collection, but bear in mind that with
collections which don't have any defined order (**Bag, Set,
Dictionary**), the elements will be processed in an unpredictable
order. Usually this doesn't matter, but be careful you don't do
something which relies on processing the elements in a particular order,
or in an order which is repeatable.

It is *very important* not to modify the collection you are
enumerating whilst you are iterating over it. This means you must not
add, or remove elements from the collection (it is fine to modify the
elements *themselves*). It is all too easy to write code like:

```
Fruits do: [:fruit | fruit isOrange ifTrue:
                            [Fruits remove: fruit]].
```

which attempts, quite reasonably, to remove all fruits which are oranges
from **Fruits**. This will not work as expected, since it is changing the
size of the collection **Fruits** as it goes along, giving unpredictable
results. If you want to perform this kind of operation, you should iterate
over **Fruits** building up a new collection containing all the fruits
which are not oranges and then replace the old collection with the new
one.

collect:

Another enumerator is **collect:** which is like **do:** except that it
builds up a new collection which contains all the results of performing
the same operation on each element in the collection. For example the
expression:

```
Names := People collect: [:person | person name].
```

would create a new collection (**Names**) containing the results of
sending the message **name** to each element in the collection **People**.
The new collection which is created will usually have the same class as
the collection which was enumerated. So if **People** was an
OrderedCollection, **Names** would be an **OrderedCollection** as
well.

select:

Next, we have **select:** which creates a new collection of just those elements of the enumerated collection which made the block true. This actually does what we wanted above. The expression:

```
Oranges := Fruits select: [:fruit | fruit isOrange].
```

would collect into **Oranges** all the fruits which answered **true** to the message **isOrange**. The opposite is **reject:** which collects all the elements which make the block **false**.

detect:

Easily confused with the other iterators is **detect:**, which stops the enumeration as soon as the first element which makes the block return **true** has been found, and returns that element. If **detect:** doesn't find such an element it generates an error. Use **detect:ifNone:** to avoid this. For example the code:

```
Winner := Employees
        detect: [:worker | worker age > 60]
        ifNone: [Employees last].
```

would pick out the first employee whose age was greater than sixty. If nobody was older than sixty, the last employee in the collection would be returned.

inject:into:

The last enumerator, **inject:into:** is rather more complicated than the others. It allows the result of executing the block using the previous element to be 'injected' into the block for the next element. The classic example sums all the values in a collection of numbers:

```
Total := Numbers inject: 0 into:
            [:subTotal :number| subTotal + number].
```

It is not trivial to understand how this works, and in practice **inject:into:** is not nearly so frequently used as the other enumerators so don't worry if it doesn't make much sense. Don't worry either if you can never remember the name of the enumerator you want, or you pick the wrong one the first time. Even experienced Smalltalk programmers have to browse the **Collection** class (**enumerating** protocol) to remind themselves which one they need!

Summary

The collection classes form a large and complex hierarchy under the class **Collection**. However, out of all the collection classes in the system you will probably find yourself using only about five or six on a regular basis. You can use collections to group together diverse sets of objects, and to implement some basic control structures (enumerating and looping).

Some of what we've discussed will become very familiar to you, and whilst you may forget the details of the rest, as long as you remember the *types* of feature that exist you'll be able to use the facilities of the various code browsers to track down the details when you need them.

The collection classes are some of the most useful in the system, and we have laboured some of the details for that reason. However, the basic features of inserting, retrieving, removing, testing for and enumerating elements are common to all collections and are well worth exploring and remembering.

Finally, the whole collection hierarchy forms a good example of how to *abstract* behaviour into superclasses, and share code among classes using inheritance. We'll be discussing how to use inheritance in Part II, and coming back to look at the collection classes and how they're implemented would be a good idea then. In the meantime, we'll continue our more detailed look into the class library by considering the *dependency mechanism*.

The Dependency Mechanism

The Smalltalk system is essentially an application *framework* upon which you as a programmer build your own application. As such it provides a number of classes which are highly reusable (both by instantiating them and by inheriting from them), and we've looked at some of those classes in the preceding chapters.

In this chapter, we are going to look not at a single class, or even a set of classes, but at a part of the framework which runs throughout the system. It is not confined to just some classes, but is available for use in *all* classes. It's available for use in your code, but is also heavily used in the system code. Most importantly, it's the basis for Smalltalk's 'Model–View–Controller' (MVC) architecture which we'll look at in the next chapter.

The subject of this chapter is the *dependency mechanism*. This mechanism may at first seem to be a rather bizarre and covert way for objects to communicate with each other. However, after reading this chapter and the next, you should have a good idea of why Smalltalk introduces such a mechanism, and understand how you can make good use of it in your own code.

The Concept of Dependency

In previous chapters we have discussed a number of the different kinds of relationship which can exist between objects. We've looked at *inheritance*, which is a relationship between a class and its subclasses. We have looked at *instantiation*, which is a relationship between an instance and its class. We've also looked at how the instance variables of one object can 'point to' or 'contain' other objects. The fourth

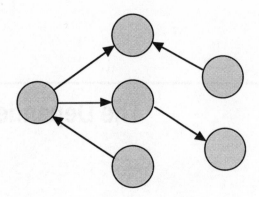

Although dependency is a one-way relationship, objects can both be dependent and have dependents. Each object can take part in as many dependency relationships as necessary.

important kind of relationship between Smalltalk objects, and the relationship which we're going to concentrate on here, is called *dependency*.

Dependency is a relationship which can be used by a programmer to connect *any* two objects together. We'll see exactly why shortly. As the diagram above illustrates, each individual object can take part in as many dependency relationships as the programmer wants. When two objects are related by dependency, we say that one object is *dependent on* or *is a dependent of* the other.

In the diagram below, object B is dependent on (or is a dependent of) object A. Looking at it the other way around, object A has object B as one of its dependents. The relationship is asymmetric. That is, just because B is dependent on A doesn't mean A is a dependent of B. It might be a dependent—it's just that that would be a separate relationship.

All this terminology can sound very confusing. Thankfully, the words are used in ways which are entirely consistent with normal English. If you're ever confused, a few moments careful thought *should* help you work out which way around a particular relationship is.

Dependency is a relationship between any kinds of object.

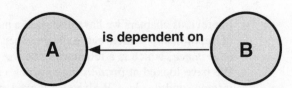

So *why* do we want objects to be dependent on each other? The reason has to do with *change*. Very often, a change in the value of an instance variable in one object will be of great interest to another object. The dependency mechanism gives objects a way of communicating changes in the values of their instance variables to their *dependents*. You can think of the dependents as being interested parties, who want to know whenever the objects on which they are dependent change the values of their instance variables.

A word of warning before we go on to look at how the dependency mechanism actually works, and show you how to use it. The dependency mechanism can be very mystifying at times—even to experienced Smalltalkers. Sometimes it can look as if objects are getting to know about changes in other objects by magic. This is never the case. Like other forms of magic, it only appears that way if you don't understand clearly what's going on.

Dependency is used by some of the classes in the class library, especially the MVC classes as we shall see. If you reuse these classes, you will be implicitly using dependency, and it should all work correctly without you having to get involved. It'll be like magic. The same applies if you use *VisualWorks* to construct your user-interface.

However, if you extend or subclass the MVC classes (perhaps to create new kinds of user-interface widget), or you want to use dependency for other reasons in your own classes (and you should feel free to do both), you will need to set up dependency relationships and call the right methods for the mechanism to work correctly. In effect you will need to be the magician. The next section tells you how to go about doing this.

How Dependency Works

The dependency mechanism is implemented by a set of methods defined in the class **Object**. This means that every object in the system can take part in dependency relationships. Some methods are *re-implemented* to do the same thing in different ways lower down in the hierarchy for efficiency or other reasons. Don't let this confuse you if you browse the classes to see how dependency works (as you should). The mechanism might work differently internally, but you use it in exactly the same way.

Every object has a collection of other objects which are its dependents. To get hold of this collection just send the message **dependents** to the object. Sometimes, the dependents are held in an instance variable inherited from above. In this case you'll be able to see it via an inspector. Other times (actually, whenever the default mechanism inherited from **Object** is being used), the dependents are held elsewhere (in a class variable in fact), and you won't be able to see them directly in an inspector. However, the message **dependents** will always give you the dependents, or **nil** if there are none. You can evaluate **self dependents** in an inspector to see the object's dependents.

To make an object become dependent on another object use **addDependent:**. The following expression will make **myObject** a dependent of **yourObject**:

```
yourObject addDependent: myObject.
```

Look very carefully at which way around this expression is. An object holds a collection of dependents. That is, an object holds a list of objects which are dependent upon it. It *does not* hold a list of objects *on which it depends*. An object *does not know* on which other objects it depends. It only knows which objects *depend on it*. This seems more confusing than it is, but you will find that it's important to remember which way around a dependency relationship is working.

To make an object no longer be a dependent of another object use **removeDependent:**. The following expression will make **myObject** no longer a dependent of **yourObject**:

```
yourObject removeDependent: myObject.
```

You will find the three methods described above in the **dependents access** protocol of **Object**, along with some other more complex, but less useful methods. Now that we know how to set up dependencies let's look at how to make them work.

Remember that the whole point of dependency is to let one object (the dependent) know when another object changes. There are two sets of methods which accomplish this feat. There is a set we shall call 'changed' methods, and a set we shall call 'update' methods. The diagram over the page shows the relationship between these methods.

Here is the crux of the dependency mechanism. Whenever an object is sent a 'changed' message, it will *automatically* send all its dependents an 'update' message. Of course like everything in Smalltalk this automatic behaviour is not hidden. It's there for you to see in the **changing** protocol of **Object**. For most practical purposes though, you can consider it as magic. When an object receives a 'changed' message all its dependents will magically receive an 'update' message.

What is not magic however is the sending of the 'changed'

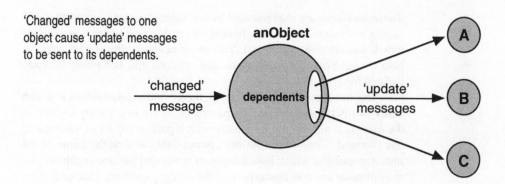

'Changed' messages to one object cause 'update' messages to be sent to its dependents.

message. If you change an object and you want its dependents to know, a 'changed' message must be sent to the changed object. Sometimes this happens in code you inherit, and sometimes you do it yourself. Either way, if you want to communicate a change, you must make sure a 'changed' message is sent. Likewise, if you want dependent objects to do something when the object on which they are dependent changes, you must implement an 'update' method.

There is a default implementation of the 'update' methods in **Object**. These methods do essentially nothing and are there to make sure you don't get an error if you send a 'changed' message to an object which has a dependent which doesn't implement an 'update' method. It just inherits the default definition and safely does nothing.

So, to make dependency work, you must *send* 'changed' messages, and *implement* 'update' methods to catch the resulting 'update' messages. Again rather confusing. You send a message of one type to one object, and another object receives a different message. Let's look in more detail at these two types of message.

'Changed' Messages

There are three different 'changed' messages, which take zero, one or two parameters. Remember, these messages are not telling an object *to* change, they are telling it that it *has* changed, and informing it that it should tell its dependents. Which one of the three messages you choose depends only on how much information you wish to communicate about the change. For example:

```
anObj changed: anAspect with: aParm.   (two parameters)
anObj changed: anAspect.   (one parameter)
anObj changed.   (no parameters)
```

These messages are implemented in the **changing** protocol of **Object** (along with some more complicated ones which we won't consider but which you are free to explore). You never have to reimplement or override them. You just send them and rely on the behaviour already defined for you.

The most powerful of these methods is **changed:with:** which takes two parameters. The first parameter is conventionally known as the *aspect*. It allows you to specify which part or *aspect* of **anObject** has changed. Very often (but not always), this will be the name of the instance variable which has changed. The second parameter allows you to communicate *how* that aspect of the object aspect has changed. Very often (but again, not always), this will be the new *value* of the instance variable.

The other two methods (**changed:** and **changed**) are *convenience* methods. They are exactly equivalent to sending **changed:with:** using **nil** for either **aParameter**, or **anAspect** *and* **aParameter**. If you look at their definitions in **Object** you will see that this is the case. Using them can just make your code slightly more readable.

'Update' Messages

Just like the 'changed' message, there are also three different 'update' messages, which take one, two, or three parameters. Remember, you will never *directly* send these messages. However, they will be *received* by your objects if other objects on which they depend are sent 'changed' messages. Exactly which one is received depends in a sense on which ones you've implemented. This may seem peculiar, but it comes about because the inherited versions of these methods actually *subsume* each other. This means that unless they're over-ridden, each method will simply call the next simplest. Here are the three update methods:

```
dependent update: anAspect with: aParm from: anObj.
dependent update: anAspect with: aParm.
dependent update: anAspect.
```

The first message is the most powerful. If you've implemented it, it is the message your object will receive whenever another object on which it is dependent receives *any* of the 'changed' messages. The values of **anAspect** and **aParameter** will be those used in the 'changed' message, or **nil** if one of the simpler 'changed' messages was used. The value of **anObject** is the object which was sent the 'changed' message, which is included so that you'll know where the 'update' message came from.

If you don't implement the **update:with:from:** method, your class will inherit the default implementation from **Object**. This simply calls **update:with:** in case you've implemented that in your class. Here you get access to the same parameters, except that you don't see where the update came from (**anObject**).

If you haven't implemented an **update:with:** method, the default implementation (which is inherited from **Object**) will call **update:**. Here you only get access to **anAspect**. If you don't implement an **update:** method the default implementation simply does nothing but return. Notice that there is no **update** method. Don't try implementing one in the hope that it will get called with no parameters. It won't!

You can see that **update:with:** and **update:** are convenience versions of **update:with:from:**. They may seem rather pointless, but the usual Smalltalk style is to use the version which takes only as many parameters as you actually need. This makes your code slightly more readable.

The diagram on the next page summarises what we have discussed, and shows how simpler 'changed' methods call more complex ones, while more complex 'update' methods call simpler ones. Ultimately, unless an object understands at least one of these 'update' messages, nothing will happen.

How Dependency is Used

The 'changed' and 'update' messages we have just looked at can be used in all sorts of different ways. However, the most common use is to let a dependent object know that the value of a single instance variable in another object has been changed.

We have talked before about using a method to *access* an instance variable in another object. Now, if inside the 'set' method (for example **size:**), the object sends *itself* a 'changed' message after setting the value of the instance variable, all the object's dependents will get to know about the change. Here is a very common method definition which does just that:

```
size: aNumber
    size := aNumber.
    self changed: #size.
```

How the various
'changed' and
'update' messages
call each other.

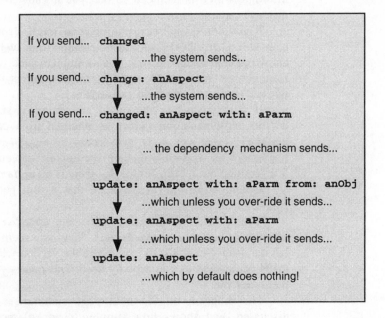

If you send...   **changed**

...the system sends...

If you send...   **change: anAspect**

...the system sends...

If you send...   **changed: anAspect with: aParm**

... the dependency mechanism sends...

update: anAspect with: aParm from: anObj

...which unless you over-ride it sends...

update: anAspect with: aParm

...which unless you over-ride it sends...

update: anAspect

...which by default does nothing!

Notice how, after setting the value of the **size** variable, the object sends itself the message **changed:** with the symbol **#size** as a parameter. This symbol is passed on to the dependents via the 'update' messages and is used to indicate which variable changed. Note that this use of the name of an instance variable as a symbol is pure convention. The parameter passed could be *any object* (not just a symbol). This is a very powerful feature which you will come to find very useful as you program in Smalltalk more.

Here is an example method definition for an 'update' method in a different class which might be invoked by the dependency mechanism following the 'changed' method above:

```
update: anAspect
    anAspect = #colour ifTrue: [self redraw].
    anAspect = #size ifTrue: [self resize].
```

This 'update' method is designed to cope with two kinds of change to objects on which it is dependent. If it's the colour that's changed it does one thing, and if it's the size it does another. Any other kind of change would be ignored.

This simple example illustrates how dependency works. You will find that by using the *aspect* and the *parameter* creatively you'll be able to come up with much more complex and powerful ways of using dependency. It's a good idea to try building some small test classes to check out your understanding of dependency. Use a workspace to make instances of your classes, make them dependent on each other, send them 'changed' messages and watch the results of your 'update' methods being called.

The class library is a good place to look for examples of the way dependency can be used. Try browsing the senders of the 'changed' messages, and the implementors of the 'update' messages to get started. If you do this, you will in fact come across many of the classes which are the subject of the next chapter.

Summary—Why Have Dependency?

The dependency mechanism is a general-purpose, reusable way of arranging for one object to know about changes to another object. Objects which are interested in changes register their interest by becoming *dependent* on the objects they're interested in changes to. When those objects change, provided they are sent (or send to themselves) a 'changed' message, then an 'update' message will be sent to all interested objects (the dependents) allowing them to do whatever they want to as a result.

You might ask the question 'Why not just arrange for an object which changes to send a message directly to another object telling it about the change?' The answer is that at the time you are writing a particular class you may *know* that other objects will be interested in changes in your objects, but you don't know *which* other objects or *how many* of them there will be. This means you can't send explicit messages to well-known objects saying 'I have changed'. What you do instead is announce that you have changed (by sending yourself a 'changed' message), and let the dependency mechanism inform those objects who have said at run-time that they're interested in knowing about the change (your dependents) that the change has occurred (by sending them an 'update' message).

In this way, the dependency mechanism can be more dynamic than hard-coding messages between objects could ever be. It also permits a sort of naivety among objects about who is interested in them. Although this sounds bad, it actually helps the encapsulation, or partitioning of functionality, which OOP encourages. This in turn greatly enhances the reusability of classes which use dependency to inform interested parties that something about themselves has changed.

This run-time registration of interest, and strong encapsulation, are also two of the features of probably the largest user of the dependency mechanism in the standard Smalltalk system. The Smalltalk graphical user-interface is based around an architecture which makes explicit and frequent use of 'change' and 'update' messages. This architecture is called Model–View–Controller, or MVC, and it's the subject of the next chapter.

The MVC Architecture

One of the most talked about, but least understood aspects of Smalltalk is the so-called *MVC* architecture. MVC (which stands for *Model–View–Controller*) has been confusing beginners since Smalltalk first appeared. This is unfortunate because it is also one of the most powerful and useful architectural features of the class library. It is in fact the basis for the point-and-click user-interface which Smalltalk uses.

If you use the *VisualWorks* GUI tools to build your user-interfaces, you are to some extent insulated from the details of MVC. It is however, still very useful to have at least an appreciation of the structures which *VisualWorks* is constructing for you. Sooner or later you will want to explore user-interfaces beyond those which *VisualWorks* can easily generate. In these cases a good understanding of the principles of MVC is essential.

The goal of this chapter is to explain clearly and concisely what MVC is about, how it works and how to use it. Don't be put off by what you may have read before, or by what you might have heard. Although at first it sounds complicated, MVC soon becomes second nature. However, before trying to understand MVC you must have a reasonable understanding of the dependency mechanism on which it relies. Provided you have read and understood the previous chapter though, you should have no problems in this respect.

Like many parts of this book, this chapter will consider the *architecture* of MVC, but won't go into great depth on how it is implemented. If you need details about the various kinds of class which are available (and which change from version to version), go to the manual, or better still browse the class hierarchy.

Basic Concepts

The description MVC describes a particular way of building applications which incorporate graphical user-interfaces. These days we are all familiar with windows, icons, push-buttons and so on—all driven by a mouse or some other pointing device. However when Smalltalk was created, such interfaces were only just being invented. Smalltalk's designers had to come up with a way of implementing a graphical user-interface in a way which would be extendable. MVC is what they came up with.

The basic premise behind the MVC architecture is that the user-interface of an application should be separated from the application functionality itself. Sometimes this is done in conventional (non-object-oriented) programs and sometimes it is not. Some object-oriented programs don't do it either, but it's not difficult to see the justification for advocating this separation.

Separating the application from its UI allows them to be *developed* separately. More importantly, it allows a new and different UI to be easily connected to an existing application. It also allows components of an existing UI to be reused on a new application. Finally, it allows an application to be used without its UI, perhaps by another application. The diagram below shows these options. You can see that all these justifications are related to the modularity, reusability and encapsulation which object-orientation promotes.

By separating the application logic from the UI, an application can have several user-interfaces, or none.

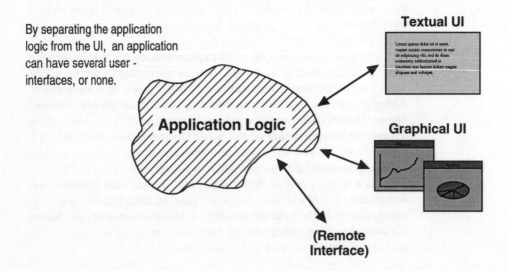

In Smalltalk, this separation of an application into its functionality and its user-interface is accomplished by using separate objects to implement the two parts. The most important objects on the application functionality side are referred to as *models*. They are the M in MVC. The most important objects on the user-interface side are referred to as *views* and *controllers*. They are the V and the C in MVC.

The class library actually provides three classes called **Model**, **View** and **Controller**. Most objects which are behaving as models, views, or controllers (and we'll see what that means shortly), inherit from one of these base classes. This isn't always the case though, especially for models, so don't let that confuse you. What's important in MVC is whether an object is *behaving* like a model or a view or a controller, not whether it necessarily *inherits* from **Model**, **View**, or **Controller**. Of course, every Smalltalk program also contains lots of objects which aren't models, views, or controllers. Don't get the impression these are not important—they are, it's just that they're not the subject of this chapter!

The MVC Architecture

The MVC architecture divides an application up into objects we can think about as being of three types: models, views and controllers. Let's start by taking a look at what each of these kinds of object are for, and how they interact with the other kinds.

Models

Models implement application functionality. They are responsible for holding the data which is relevant to the application, and acting upon it in the ways the application defines. They can be very simple (for example, an instance of class **String** can be a model), or very complex (perhaps an entire word processing application). Very often, several model objects will work together to implement the application, and we'll see a particular way of arranging this later.

What matters is that models hold the data, and act upon it in ways which are *independent* of the user-interface. This allows different user-interfaces, or other objects, to use the model functionality. You can start to see a similarity to the naivety we talked about when discussing the dependency mechanism.

Views

Views present information to the user. They are responsible for taking the data held in model objects and displaying it on the screen in the form of text, graphics, widgets and so on. However, views don't 'understand' the data. Neither do they act upon it, except in the ways necessary to display it.

The class library provides all sorts of different views. These allow you to display the data in your models in all sorts of different ways, *without having to change the models*. You will find that there are views for everything, from whole windows to scrollbar buttons. A single window almost always contains many view objects cooperating together to create the user-interface.

Controllers

Views are responsible for the output, or display side of the user-interface. *Controllers* on the other hand, are responsible for handling input. They 'listen' to the keyboard and mouse, and interpret input from both in terms of how the model must be manipulated. Again, the system class library contains many different controller classes. Each one of these controllers is usually specialised to work with one or more types of view. Controllers are always paired up with views, but they tend to be the 'poor relation' of the two. Wherever there's a view though, there's usually a controller lurking in the background.

Putting MVC Together

You should now have a basic idea of how the models, views and controllers in an application work together to implement the application's functionality, present it to the user and allow the user to interact with the application. As the next diagram shows, models, views and controllers tend to form little 'triads' of co-operating objects. Each model object is interfaced to the screen, keyboard and mouse by a view object and a controller object.

Sadly, the partitioning of functionality among models, views and controllers, is not an exact science. Sometimes, 'view-like' functionality leaks into models when they have to know something about exactly how they're being presented on the screen. At other times, 'model-like' functionality leaks into controllers, where it is more convenient to deal with mouse-clicks and so on. Don't worry too much about this. The important thing when designing a system, and deciding

The views and controllers work together to control the user-interface to the models.

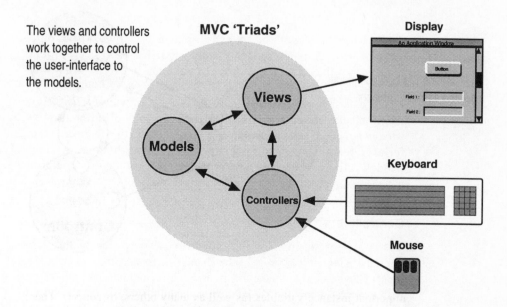

MVC 'Triads'

what to put where, is to try to remember *why* functionality should be split the way it is. Keeping in mind the normal OOP goals of modularity, reusability and encapsulation should help you to make the right decisions.

MVC Details

Now that we've looked at the principles behind MVC, and considered its basic architecture, we will look at *some* of the details behind how it is implemented in *VisualWorks*. If you're interested in understanding *all* the details you should look in your manual, or browse the system code. Be wary though if you are familiar with programming in another window system. Smalltalk works quite differently from MS-Windows, the X window system or the Macintosh. In particular, the window system is *polled*, not event-driven. This may change in the future, but for now you should be aware that it makes programming with the Smalltalk UI different from most other window systems.

Look carefully at the next diagram. It shows the relationships between the model, view and controller objects. The view has two very

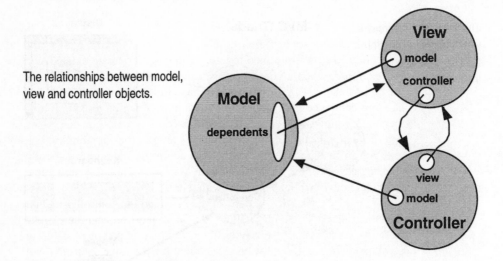

The relationships between model, view and controller objects.

important instance variables (as well as many others, of course). There is a variable called **model** which contains the model the view is displaying, and a variable called **controller**, which contains the controller used to modify the model when the user uses the mouse or keyboard to interact with the system. The view also has variables which point to its 'container' in the window (the larger view it is probably a part of), and to its 'components' (the things it in turn contains).

Similarly, the controller has two important instance variables shown in the above diagram—**model** and **view**. These variables contain (or 'point to' if you prefer to think of it in that way) the model and the view objects respectively.

Notice how the view and the controller are fully aware of each other's existence, and of the existence of the model. This means that the view is able to ask the model (because it knows which object it is) for the data it is supposed to be displaying on the screen. Likewise, the controller is able to send the model messages telling it to perform operations when commanded by the user through the mouse or keyboard.

The model *does not have* instance variables containing the view or the controller (it has plenty of others of course!). Instead, the view has made itself a dependent of the model. This means that (provided the model uses the 'changed' messages which are part of the dependency mechanism) the view will get to know if the model changes in some way, and can reflect the result on the screen. The model meanwhile, remains blissfully ignorant of which view or *views* are being used to display it.

This arrangement has a number of effects. Firstly, views and controllers are tightly linked together and can co-operate extensively. For example, when a controller receives a mouse-click, it may know the co-ordinates of the click, but will have to ask the view what object is being displayed there, in order to decide what action to take. It also means that views and controllers always come in pairs. In fact, when you make an instance of one of the many views in the class library, you will get an instance of the appropriate controller class automatically attached to it, without really noticing it. Most views in the system know what class of controller should go with them.

You might ask why the jobs of the view and the controller are not combined into a single object. This is a good question, and there are at least two answers. First, having them separate makes it possible to combine them in different ways. You might use the same controller, but change the view to display the model's data differently (to get a different *look*). Alternatively, you might use the same kind of view, but change its controller to work differently with the mouse (to get a different *feel*).

The other answer to the question is that separating the view and the controller allows them to *inherit* from different classes. This means that the view functionality and the controller functionality can be structured quite differently in the class hierarchy. This technique of composing functionality from combinations of instances is actually one way of overcoming Smalltalk's lack of 'multiple-inheritance' (where a class can inherit not just from one direct superclass, but from several superclasses at the same level).

The other result of the way the model, view and controller are structured is that the model is not directly aware of the view (or of the controller for that matter). This means that a different view/controller combination could be plugged into the model to display and interact with it differently, without the model having to be changed at all. Also, because dependency is used to connect the view to the model, the model can in fact have *more* than one view/controller at the same time. As many views as want to, can become dependent on the model, and display its data simultaneously. They will all receive 'update' messages whenever the model changes (provided it sends itself the right 'changed' messages of course), and they will all know to redraw themselves if necessary as a result of the change.

The messages which pass between model, view and controller.

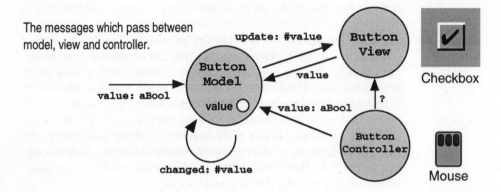

MVC in Action

The preceding sections have explained the concepts behind MVC and described how models, views and controllers are connected together. This section completes the picture by showing how MVC works at run-time. We'll use a very simple example—a checkbox which can be either 'on' or 'off'. The classes and methods are fictional to make them very simple, but this simple example illustrates the concepts which more complex models, views and controllers build upon.

The diagram above shows the three MVC objects. There is a model (**ButtonModel**) which has a single boolean variable—one that can take one of only two values, **true** or **false**. This variable is called **value**. There is a view (**ButtonView**) which is responsible for producing a graphical representation of the state of the **value** variable in **ButtonModel**, in the form of a three-dimensional widget on the screen. Finally, there is a controller object (**ButtonController**) which is responsible for changing the state of the **value** variable in **ButtonModel** whenever the view's button widget is clicked on by the user. The following might be a typical sequence of events in the life of these objects:

1. The window in which **ButtonView** is sitting is opened and so **ButtonView** has to draw the widget for the first time. To determine the correct look (pressed in or popped out), the view sends the model the message **value**. The return value from this message will be either **true** or **false**, and the view uses this information to decide how to draw the widget.

2. The user comes along and clicks the mouse on the area of the screen managed by **ButtonView**. The **ButtonController** sees this, and enters into a dialogue with **ButtonView** to determine if the click was actually within the checkbox widget. If it was, the controller must send a message to the model to tell it to invert its state (become **true** if it was **false**, and vice versa). Now, the controller doesn't know the current state of the model so it evaluates something like: **model value : model value not**. If you think very carefully about this expression, and remember the rules of precedence, you'll see that the controller is asking the model for its value (using **model value**), inverting it (**not**), and sending the result back to the model (**value :**).

3. The model has now been changed, and as part of its **value:** method it sends *itself* the message **changed: #value**. This causes an 'update' to go out to all the model's dependents informing them that an object upon which they are dependent has changed.

4. The **ButtonView**, being one of the model's dependents, receives the update in the form of the **update: #value** message. Its implementation of **update:** simply re-executes the code that it used to draw the widget in the first place. This sends the message **value** to the model to find out the new value, and then draws the widget appropriately.

You should try to remember a number of important points from this example. First, neither the view nor the controller hold onto the model's state (**true** or **false**). Every time they need it, they ask for it. Second, the controller doesn't know anything about the visual layout of the widget. When it needs that information, it asks the view. Third, when the controller changes the state of the model, it doesn't directly tell the view. Fourth, the model doesn't know about the view. When its state is changed by the controller, it's only because of the dependency mechanism that the view gets to know about the change. Finally, when the model tells the view that it's changed (using dependency), it doesn't tell the view the new state—it only tells it what *aspect* has changed (**#value**, meaning that the instance variable called **value** has changed). The view has to ask the model for the new state of that variable.

We can now imagine that this example could be extended in a number of different ways. **ButtonModel** could start holding more information than just a boolean variable. For example, it could hold the string which would be used by the view to label the checkbox. **ButtonView** would then have to send an additional message to retrieve the label from the model before displaying it. Also, instead of executing **self changed: #value** to let its dependents know it has changed, **ButtonModel** could be more helpful by executing **self changed: #value with: self value**. This would pass the new value of the **value** variable directly on to the dependents, thus avoiding the need for them having to ask for it.

Finally, notice how the diagram shows that an unknown 'third party' (not **ButtonController**) could also change the state of **ButtonModel** by sending it a **value:** message. To the model, this is indistinguishable from the controller doing it, and so the dependency mechanism still kicks in, allowing the view to reflect the new state of the model correctly.

An Extension to MVC

We have now completed our discussion of the 'classic' MVC architecture of Smalltalk. If you have understood the principles, even partly, you've understood what many people consider to be the most difficult part of programming in Smalltalk. However, the *VisualWorks* system extends the notion of MVC very slightly. It does this both to reflect the best practices in using MVC established over the years, and to make MVC more 'pluggable' (a topic we'll address in the next chapter).

The basic modification is to split the model part of MVC into two pieces. These are usually referred to as the *data model*, and the *application model*. This split reflects the dual role which many model objects have—they act as a store for the application's data, and they act upon that data in application specific ways. The diagram on the next page shows what the resulting architecture looks like. If you build your application's user-interface using the *VisualWorks* tools, you will construct an architecture that looks similar to this.

Splitting the model in this way removes application specific processing from the data model, making it much more reusable. It also provides something of a justification for putting some user-interface functionality in the application model. After all, in some cases an application is nothing more than a particular set of operations with a particular user-interface. Consequently, it does not matter *too much* if the application model knows some things about the user-interface. In this case the application *is* the interface.

Data Models

The MVC's model objects can be split into an application model and several data models.

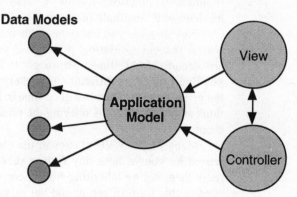

Making this split also allows the different types of model to inherit from different places. Typically, *data* models are things like collection objects, strings, numbers, booleans, files and so on. In other words, they're instances of some of the basic 'data structure' classes in the system being used to do what they do best—store and manipulate data in general ways.

On the other hand, typical *application* models are objects representing things like browsers, dialogs, editors and the like. When you create classes like these in *VisualWorks*, they will usually inherit from **ApplicationModel**. This is a class which provides the basic hooks for creating such application models in the *VisualWorks* environment.

Summary

Although sometimes a source of much confusion, MVC is really not as difficult to understand and use as Smalltalk mythology might have you believe. One way of looking at the MVC architecture is as a *framework*. Rather than having to architect every Smalltalk program from scratch, MVC gives you a ready-designed architecture exactly suited to building applications with graphical user-interfaces. It then goes on to give you a whole range of classes (models, views and controllers) which work with this architecture, and which you can reuse in your own programs.

The architecture is based around a few simple principles, mainly the notion of encapsulation—the separation of *application* and *data* (model) functionality from *presentation* (view) and *interaction* (controller) functionality. MVC also makes use of an important mechanism in Smalltalk (dependency).

Provided that you understand this mechanism, and you try to work within the encapsulation principles, you will find that the MVC architecture works almost like magic to support your programming. If you find yourself in difficulty, it is likely that you're trying go 'against the grain' of MVC. That's a good time to look again at your design, and think about whether it is obeying the principles we've discussed in this chapter.

Many of the MVC classes in the class library are designed to be reused by you without any further subclassing. In other words, you reuse them not by inheriting from them, but by instantiating them. To support this form of reuse, and yet retain maximum flexibility, these classes make use of a concept called 'pluggability'. As we've just observed, when you use *VisualWorks* to build an application, the resulting code will have separate application and data models. *VisualWorks* actually connects these models together using objects called 'adaptors'. The two concepts of pluggability and adaptors are therefore the subject of the next chapter.

Chapter

10

Pluggability and Adaptors

One of the key benefits of object-oriented programming is *reuse*. The
ability to make use of someone else's code (especially that in the class
library) and to write your own reusable classes, is what makes OOP
more productive than conventional programming. This seems obvious,
but in fact there are several ways to reuse existing code.

The first form of reuse we tend to think of when doing OOP is
inheritance. This allows you to define new classes simply by specifying
how they differ from existing classes. Since the differences are
normally much smaller than the overall functionality, a great efficiency
gain is thereby made.

A somewhat less obvious but in Smalltalk more frequent form of
reuse is to simply make instances of existing classes and use them
without inheritance. Whenever you use numbers, strings, collections,
widgets and all the rest of the classes in the library you are doing
precisely this.

A third form of reuse is to treat Smalltalk like a software
constructor kit, and 'plug' instances of existing classes into each other,
without actually writing any classes of your own. This is the technique
which the *VisualWorks* GUI tools rely on very effectively.

The last two forms of reuse can give rise to a problem. When you
make instances of collection classes for example, you (the programmer)
know the protocol (the set of messages) they support and can write your
code appropriately. However the writers of the UI widget classes had
no idea what protocol your classes would understand, and so couldn't
specialise the widgets to work with them. Similarly, treating Smalltalk
as a constructor kit means that all the components have to be able to
plug into each other, and so must be configurable in ways which could
not have been anticipated when the classes were written.

Fortunately, there are a couple of mechanisms in Smalltalk (blocks and **perform:** methods) which allow programmers to build in the kind of flexibility needed to overcome these problems. There are many classes in the class library which take advantage of this, and it is just some of these classes which are the subject of this chapter.

The notion of pluggability, and the classes which support it, are worth studying for a couple of reasons. First, they form the basis of the *VisualWorks* GUI tools. Although *VisualWorks* does its best to hide you from the complexities involved, there are times when if your code doesn't work the way you expected, you will have to lift the lid and find out why! Second, the programming techniques involved illustrate some of the most powerful features of Smalltalk—features which you will find invaluable in trying to write your own reusable classes.

To understand the message of this chapter, you need to understand the mechanisms on which pluggability is based: blocks and **perform:** . We looked at blocks in Chapter 4—*The Smalltalk Language*, so we'll start here with an introduction to **perform:** .

The **perform:** Mechanism

In chapter 4 we looked at the syntax for sending messages to objects. To send a message to an object you just name the object and then type the message you want to send to it. For example:

```
MyObject reset.
```

When this code is run the system looks up the class of **MyObject** and calls the appropriate implementation of the method **reset** for that class. You might remember that this run-time lookup of the method is what gives rise to *polymorphism*—different objects responding differently to the same message. This is a very powerful feature of object-oriented programming, but in Smalltalk even this flexibility is sometimes not enough.

In the example above, the implementation of **reset** to be used is not known until *run-time*, but the name of the method is known at *compile-time* (when the method is saved using **accept** in a browser). However, sometimes even the name of the method can only be decided at run-time. For cases like this Smalltalk provides a set of methods called **perform:** and its derivatives. These methods allow you to tell an object to execute a method whose name, rather than being hard-coded as above, is sent as a parameter. This means that the name of the method need not be known until run-time. For example:

```
MyObject perform: MyCommand.
```

When this expression is evaluated **MyObject** will be sent whatever message is contained in the variable **MyCommand**. This is expected to be a symbol naming a method understood by **MyObject**. So if **MyCommand** had the value **#reset**, the message **reset** would be sent to **MyObject**. Note that the name of the method needs to be a symbol, not a string.

If a message with parameters needs to be sent to an object, there are variations of the **perform:** message which can send 1, 2, 3 or a whole array of parameters. These variations are:

```
perform:with:
perform:with:with:
perform:with:with:with:
perform:withArguments:
```

This mechanism may seem rather peculiar, and indeed you should use it with caution as it is rarely needed, is less efficient, and more confusing than an ordinary message send. However, there are times when you're trying to write reusable code, when **perform:** is a powerful facility. Together with the notion of blocks, **perform:** is the basis for the pluggability which is the subject of this chapter.

Pluggability

Hopefully you can now start to see how it is possible to write classes which perform general functions, and which can be customised by giving them either a block of code (which they run by sending it the message **value**) or a symbol (which they send as a message to another object using **perform:**). The block or symbol is held in an instance variable of the class. Only the *fixed* messages **value** and **perform:** need be hard-coded by the original programmer, with the symbol or block being provided by the reuser at run-time. This effectively allows the behaviour of a pre-defined class to be modified *without* subclassing, and on an instance-by-instance (rather than a class) basis.

Several classes in the class library make use of the 'indirection' which this pluggability allows. We're going to look at just three of them—one which provides indirection without using either of the above mechanisms (**ValueHolder**), one which uses **perform:** (**AspectAdaptor**) and one which uses blocks (**PluggableAdaptor**). The diagram overleaf shows the fragment of the hierarchy into which

A portion of the class hierarchy showing subclasses of **ValueModel**, including **ValueHolder**, **AspectAdaptor** and **PluggableAdaptor**.

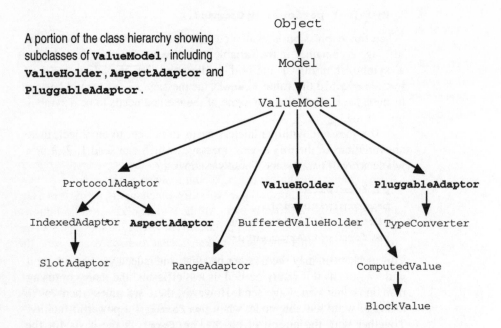

these classes fit. You can see that there are many other similar classes (some have been omitted from the diagram for clarity), and you should feel free to browse and use these classes as necessary. All the classes inherit from **ValueModel**. This fragment of the hierarchy is also a good example of the kind of abstraction which inheritance permits—generating highly reusable but sometimes a little opaque class definitions.

The general purpose of instances of all these classes is to act as connectors or *adaptors* between two other objects. The diagram below shows this in action. Adaptors translate the protocol or messages sent by each object into messages the other object understands. This is what

Adaptors allow you to connect two objects together by converting the protocols they speak.

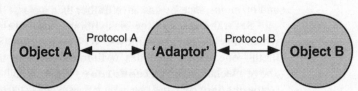

Adaptors can connect
UI objects (widgets)
which speak only
value/**value** : to
model objects with their
own protocol.

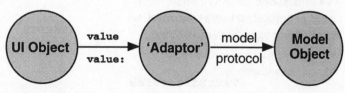

allows for example, Object A and Object B in the previous diagram to work together without having been built to do so.

The most important use for this mechanism is in the user-interfaces built by *VisualWorks*. All the widget classes (radio-buttons, text-fields, etc.) speak a fixed protocol. They send the message **value** to their model when they want to know what to display, and send the message **value:** to the model when they want to change it.

Most model objects do not understand this **value**/**value:** protocol, and so it must be converted to something they do understand. Each of the three classes we will look at does this in a different way. Each class understands the same **value**/**value:** protocol on one side, but does a different thing on the other. The diagram above shows this. Let's now look at these classes one by one.

The **ValueHolder** Class

Instances of class **ValueHolder** allow *VisualWorks* widgets to work with the simplest of models. They are basically 'wrappers' which enclose simple model objects like instances of **String**, **Number** or **Boolean**, and make them respond to **value** and **value:** instead of the more complex protocol they normally understand. Instances of **ValueHolder** are created by sending the message **asValue** to any object. Look at the implementation of **asValue** in **Object** to see this.

When a **ValueHolder** is sent the message **value**, it simply returns the object it is wrapping (its 'value'). When it is sent the message **value:** with a parameter, the **ValueHolder** throws away its original value and replaces it with the object sent as a parameter. Notice what this means. When a widget wants to 'modify' the value of its model (a **String** for example), the model isn't changed, it is *replaced*. This has important implications for anyone else using that model, and is the other reason for using a **ValueHolder**.

107

A **ValueHolder** converts a simple model for use by a widget and allows the model to be shared amongst several other objects.

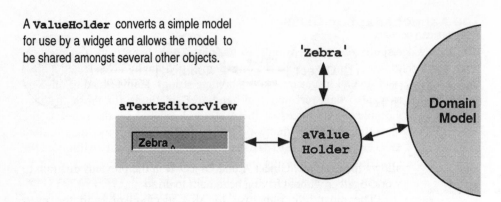

If the actual string being displayed was referenced by all the other objects interested in it, whenever it was thrown away and replaced, all these objects would have to have their references changed. However, by using a **ValueHolder** which is never replaced, all the objects using a model can just keep hold of the same **ValueHolder**, even though its value is changing. The diagram above shows how a **ValueHolder** allows a string (**' Zebra'**) to be interfaced to a **TextEditorView** and be accessed from a domain model.

In this way, instances of **ValueHolder** act as containers which stay around, even though their contents (their values) are coming and going. If you're familiar with C programming, you can think of this as being somewhat like a pointer to a pointer (don't worry if this doesn't mean anything!).

As well as acting as containers for objects, instances of **ValueHolder** can also let interested parties know when their values change. This is possible thanks to the dependency mechanism discussed in chapter 8. **ValueHolder** even provides a convenient way to connect to this using the **onChangeSend:to:** method. This allows you to ask the **ValueHolder** to send a particular message to a particular object whenever its value is replaced (which is what a change means in a **ValueHolder**). For example:

MyValHold onChangeSend: #refresh to: MyDomainModel.

This expression arranges for the message **refresh** to be sent to **MyDomainModel** every time the value of **MyValHold** is changed by being sent the message **value:**. You might like to try browsing the code to see if you can see how **ValueHolder** uses another class, **DependencyAdaptor**, to make this happen.

The `AspectAdaptor` Class

`AspectAdaptor` is similar to `ValueHolder`, but provides an interface to more complex models. For example, you might have created a class with several instance variables holding strings, numbers and so on. You may also have created 'get' and 'set' methods for those instance variables. The names of these methods should be the same as the instance variable names, so you might have methods called `insideLeg` and `insideLeg:` to get and set the value of the `insideLeg` variable (as in the diagram below). Now you want to display and edit the value of this variable in a `TextEditorView`. However, the view sends the messages `value` and `value:` when it wants to get and set the value of the object it is displaying. So, you need a way of converting these messages into the ones your class understands. This is what `AspectAdaptor` does.

In this context, the `insideLeg` variable is referred to as an 'aspect' of your model. The task of `AspectAdaptor` is to interface the general-purpose view object to just one aspect of the model. To do this, it needs to know which messages to send. The `AspectAdaptor` refers to these messages as the `getSelector` and the `putSelector` (selector is a term frequently used to refer to a message name). When you make an `AspectAdaptor` you can either set these two messages at the same time using the `forAspect:` message (in which case the `getSelector` will be set to the symbol you give, and the `putSelector` to the same symbol with a colon (`:`) appended), or (more unusually) you can set them separately using

An `AspectAdaptor` can be used to interface a view to a single 'aspect' of a complex model.

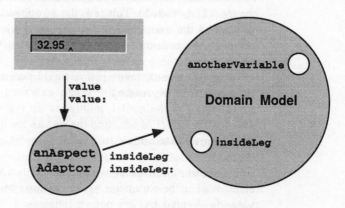

accessWith:assignWith:. You must also tell the **AspectAdaptor** which object it is adapting using the **subject:** message.

The **AspectAdaptor** will also propagate 'update' messages. To make this happen, make sure you have sent the message **subjectSendsUpdates: true** to the adaptor. Then, if the domain model changes the value of **insideLeg**, and provided it sends itself a **changed: #insideLeg** message, the **AspectAdaptor** will forward the resulting **update:** message to the view.

The **PluggableAdaptor** Class

Instances of **PluggableAdaptor** take the whole concept of pluggability a stage further than **AspectAdaptor**. Instead of merely being able to provide *selectors* to be used to adapt a model to a view, you get to provide entire *blocks* of Smalltalk code. The blocks are called the **getBlock**, the **putBlock** and the **updateBlock**. They are executed when the **PluggableAdaptor** receives the messages **value**, **value:** and **update:with:from:** respectively. This gives a great deal of flexibility in adapting a model to a view. Here is a simple example in which we wish to adapt a view to a model which holds a value in the variable **insideLeg** in inches, but we wish to display and edit it in centimetres.

```
MyPA := PluggableAdaptor on: MyModel.
MyPA getBlock: [:m | m insideLeg * 2.5]
    putBlock: [:m :v | m insideLeg: (v / 2.5)]
    updateBlock: [:m :a :p | (a = #insideLeg) & (p > 34)].
```

First, we make an instance of **PluggableAdaptor** and connect it to the model (**MyModel**). This tells the **PluggableAdaptor** what object to send as the **:m** parameter in the above blocks, and instructs it to become a dependent of that object. Then we set the values of the three blocks.

The **getBlock** takes just a single parameter, **:m** — the model (which will be **MyModel**). When executed it sends the message **insideLeg** to the model, multiplies the result by 2.5 and returns it. This has the effect of adapting the **value** message sent by the view to the **PluggableAdaptor** to a more complex operation performed on the model.

The **putBlock** takes two parameters, **:m** and **:v** — the value (the object sent as the parameter to the **value:** message). In this case, the value is divided by 2.5 before being sent to the model using the

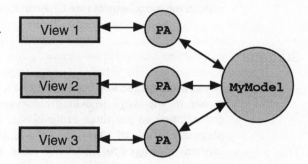

Several **P luggableAdaptor** objects being used to adapt different aspects of a single model to individual views.

insideLeg: message. This has the effect of adapting the **value:** message sent to the **PluggableAdaptor** to another complex operation performed on the model.

Finally, the **updateBlock** is executed by the **PluggableAdaptor** whenever it receives an update message from the model. This might happen if **MyModel** has changed the value of its **insideLeg** variable and sent itself the message **changed: #insideLeg with: insideLeg**. This informs all its dependents that **insideLeg** has changed its value, and sends them the new value.

The **PluggableAdaptor** must decide whether to forward this update on to its own dependents (typically a view). To make this decision, it runs the **updateBlock**. If it evaluates to **true** it forwards the update, if it evaluates to **false** it does not. If the **updateBlock** evaluates to anything else an error is generated, so be careful!

This process allows **PluggableAdaptors** to filter the many updates they might receive from their model, and forward only those that the view is interested in. This is essential because, as the diagram above shows, a given model may have many instances of **PluggableAdaptor** connected it. The model may generate an update whenever *any* of its variables changes, and *all* of the adaptors will receive these messages. If the update messages weren't filtered, all the views would refresh themselves when only one needed to. This can cause unpleasant flickering on the screen.

Instances of **PluggableAdaptor** really do lead a double life. They connect a model to a view, appearing to be like a model to the view, and like a view to the model. The code that can be placed in their blocks is essentially unlimited, and this can make them very powerful indeed. Be careful though, because code placed in blocks, and hence applying to only one instance, is invariably more difficult to debug than code in the model object (see Chapter 15—*Debugging Smalltalk Code*).

Summary

Reuse is one of the key benefits of OOP, and in Smalltalk pluggability is one of the ways in which reuse is achieved. This chapter has concentrated on just three of the classes in the class library which are pluggable. Each of these classes adapts the **value**, **value:**, and 'update' messages to something more appropriate. This means that view-like objects (buttons, text-editors, etc.) which typically send **value** and **value:** can be connected to model objects which don't directly understand these messages.

Don't worry if you haven't understood the details of what these adaptor classes do. In many cases their functionality is hidden and you needn't worry about it. As long as you have understood the general principles, you will be in a good position to work out exactly what is happening as and when you need to do so.

Many other classes in the class library are also pluggable, and you should feel free to browse them to discover how they work. Be aware though, that pluggability is one of the features that has been around in the class library for a little while, which is why there is some inconsistency in the way it is implemented, and in the way the classes are named.

Finally, if you have really understood the concepts presented in this chapter, you should find that if you need to build classes which are reused in general ways by other programmers, pluggability is one of the ways you'll consider.

Part

II

The Art of Smalltalk

Introduction to The Art of Smalltalk

In the first part of this book we looked at the 'science' of Smalltalk programming. We discussed how one of the key features of Smalltalk is that you do not have to know everything about it in order to be highly productive. The emphasis in Part I was on what you really *have* to know to get started.

If you've read and understood most of the chapters in Part I you should now have a good understanding of what an object is. You should also be familiar with the Smalltalk language, happy with the basics of the Smalltalk development environment, and know something about the most important classes and features of the Smalltalk class library. Hopefully, you will also have experimented for yourself, at least with the examples in the text, if not with more complex constructions of your own.

In theory everything else is just more of the same. With enough time and exposure you could become intimately familiar with the development environment and build up an extensive knowledge of the class library. More importantly, you would also build up the bank of personal experience which proficient Smalltalk developers use all the time to guide their design and programming activities. It is this second kind of knowledge, combined with the basic flexibility and power of Smalltalk, that makes Smalltalk programming so productive and rewarding. This kind of knowledge is the 'art' of Smalltalk.

Aims of The Art of Smalltalk

Part II of this book introduces the 'art' of Smalltalk. It is essentially a set of guidelines—giving advice which you may choose to follow as little or as much as you please. The emphasis here is on practical experience, rather than theoretical methodology. That's not to say that precise methodologies don't have a place—they do, especially in large and complex projects. However, a methodology is not necessarily a substitute for the 'common sense' and practical experience which forms the basis of *The Art of Smalltalk*.

Some of the advice given here is probably generally applicable across all object-oriented languages (if not all of programming). Since this is a book on Smalltalk though, and since you are presumably interested in how to be maximally effective in Smalltalk, most of the advice is presented specifically in the context of that language. Because of this, you're assumed to have at least a reading knowledge of Smalltalk and OOP concepts, gained either from Part I or just as valuably, from previous Smalltalk experience.

Structure of The Art of Smalltalk

We'll be splitting *The Art of Smalltalk* into several pieces. In fact, we'll follow the development cycle presented roughly in the diagram below. This is of course a classic development cycle, and it's as applicable in Smalltalk as anywhere else. The only thing that's different is how quickly you can get around the loop. In Smalltalk it's possible to traverse it very quickly indeed. How quickly you actually iterate around this cycle depends on you—it may be minutes, or it may be days,

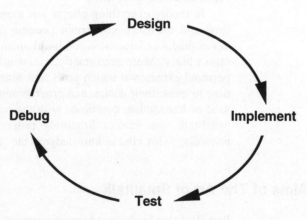

A classic development cycle —as applicable in Smalltalk as any other language, although perhaps traversed more rapidly.

Design

Implement

Test

Debug

weeks, months or even years. You will always find though that your activities can be classified according to this cycle.

The first thing we're going to look at then is designing for Smalltalk. Like many things there isn't necessarily a right or wrong way to go about doing this. What we'll do therefore is to consider some ideas and principles which might help you think about that most difficult of OO tasks—*'finding the objects'*. We'll also cover the various ways in which you can help make your classes more reusable.

One of the more important aspects of design is the use of inheritance, and so we'll consider that in some depth. It's easy to use inheritance for the wrong things in Smalltalk, but hopefully once you're aware of the various pitfalls you'll be able to avoid them.

Next we'll look at coding in Smalltalk, including using conventions that will make your code easier to maintain, and more reusable. Then we'll look at using the Smalltalk development environment for maximum efficiency. It's very easy to get stuck using just a minimal set of functionality, so this chapter tries to break that habit!

Since it's unlikely that all your programs will work first time, we'll then look at debugging in Smalltalk, which can be an art in itself. We'll also talk about a whole range of common bugs which appear in Smalltalk programs again and again, or which are particularly difficult to find, and so are worth trying to avoid.

Finally, we'll cover some of the important issues which arise in the management of a Smalltalk development project, look at how to work in a team of Smalltalk developers, and summarise the message of this book as a whole.

One of the areas we won't be covering here is *requirements analysis*. Just as in conventional programming, you must have a good understanding of the problem you are trying to solve before you try to design a system to solve it. Smalltalk doesn't make that part of the job go away. The only thing that is probably true is that the speed of system development in Smalltalk may permit you to discover *early* that you are solving the wrong problem. Likewise, the iterative nature of the development process may allow you to *change* the problem you are solving halfway through. However, just as in conventional programming, neither of these things allows you to get away with not knowing what you're trying to do at any particular time.

Sadly, the *art* of Smalltalk is probably more difficult than the *science*. Only you know exactly what you're trying to do, and so only you can decide whether the advice presented here is applicable to your situation, and if so whether even to apply it. However, if you're an

117

experienced programmer, you can take some comfort here. You should find that you can actually reuse many of your existing design and programming skills once you realise how they relate to object-oriented programming in general, and to Smalltalk programming in particular.

As we've said, there is no one 'right' way to go about designing and programming in Smalltalk. If you have a way which works well, by all means use it. What is presented here is just one developer's set of practical experiences. If you read and understand them, they should help you rapidly climb the learning curve, and help you develop your own Smalltalk experience bank. Let's now start at the beginning by considering the art of *designing* for Smalltalk.

Designing for Smalltalk

The subtitle of this chapter could easily be 'Finding the Objects'. It's all very well understanding what an object actually *is*, but it's much harder to decide what kinds of object you should *design* in order to implement an application in Smalltalk. Indeed given a set of requirements for an application and a development system like Smalltalk, 'finding the objects' is easily the most difficult task an inexperienced OO developer has to face. But then learning about concepts and techniques is always more difficult than learning about programming languages or tools.

Take heart however. If you're an experienced procedural programmer you probably find it very easy to decide what functionality to put in which procedure in order to create elegant programs. But it wasn't always that way. When you first started programming you may have found this partitioning quite hard. One way or another though, it became a natural skill. Just like splitting a program into procedures, splitting a program into objects is something that can also become a very natural skill. Sadly, it does take time and experience to acquire the skills of object-oriented design (OOD). The aim of this chapter is to help you acquire these skills more quickly.

We can't really hope to do justice to the full range and depth of OOD in one chapter. That takes whole books or more. Instead, the intention here is to give you a feel for what doing the design for systems which will be realised in Smalltalk is like. We'll look at how it is different from 'conventional' design, what the major considerations are, and what tasks OOD involves. We'll consider some ways of trying to 'find the objects' (although sadly, there will be no magic spells), and finish by looking at how to make good use of inheritance. We'll illustrate the theory with some examples, and although it's not always perfect, if you really want to see more examples of good Smalltalk design, you could do much worse than look at the classes in the system library.

How Designing for Smalltalk is Different

It's important to be aware of how the process of doing design for Smalltalk systems is different from doing conventional design. Some differences are obvious. In conventional programming, you can consider the structure of the data separately from the structure of the code which acts upon it. The very nature of OOP means that these two concepts are bound together. In Smalltalk (but not for example, in C++), every single bit of code has to be associated with a class. This in itself can cause beginners trouble.

We have discussed several times how developing in Smalltalk is an *iterative* process. This means that periods of analysis may be followed by periods of design, which may in turn be followed by prototype implementation, before further design or analysis work is undertaken. Don't let the fact that we are considering design separately—in its own chapter—convince you that iterative development or rapid-prototyping is an optional feature of Smalltalk programming. It isn't.

This iterative character means you must be very careful if you want to employ a formal process of design or use an existing architecture, especially if that process or structure has been created for conventional programming languages. Some existing methodologies emphasise a *waterfall* approach. The system is completely designed from the top down, then implemented from the bottom up. There is a good reason for this. It is very expensive to correct design mistakes when using a conventional language. However, the techniques which are useful for waterfall development tend to break down when you use them for iterative development. This is because they rely on one phase of the process being completed before the next can commence—no good for the opportunistic approach possible with Smalltalk.

Some techniques also tend to emphasise language independence. You create a design which you could then go on to implement in C, C++, Pascal, or whatever. However, one of the key benefits of using Smalltalk is being able to reuse the code in the class library. To do this you must take into account during the design process the fact that you will be implementing in Smalltalk. Do otherwise and you could end up specifying classes which are orthogonal to the way the existing class library is structured. You would then be forced to implement much more functionality than would otherwise have been needed. If design dependence on the target language seems unpalatable, think of it as being like knowing what material you plan to build a boat from at the time you design it. Just like real wood the Smalltalk class library has a 'grain'. Life will be much easier during implementation if your design goes with the grain instead of across it.

Of course there are a number of excellent, more formal, methodologies for OOD and Smalltalk. These include Hewlett Packard's *Fusion* which is a general object-oriented methodology covering all parts of the life-cycle of an object-oriented system, and ParcPlace's *Object Behavior Analysis and Design* which is specific to Smalltalk. If you are doing something other than a small- or medium-sized project, or have particular concerns about traceability or rigour in your approach to design, you would be well advised to consider adopting one of these techniques. Throughout the rest of this chapter though, we'll be talking in general terms about the concepts which many OOD approaches share, and considering how they apply to Smalltalk. These are the things which most Smalltalk programmers do or think about when engaging in the informal process of designing a Smalltalk program.

Design Considerations

When you design for a procedural language you have to ask questions like 'What procedures should I have?', 'What should they return?' and 'What should be passed as a parameter?'. When doing OOD you have to add additional questions like 'Which class should this method be in?' and 'Should I subclass or encapsulate that class?' OOP forces you to think about these issues, and in fact by doing so encourages you to do a better job of design.

OOP does not prevent bad design though. It's just as easy to create poorly structured, un-maintainable, bug-ridden applications which don't meet the requirements in an object-oriented language as it is in a conventional one. However, by being aware of what constitutes good and bad design in OOP, and having a set of skills for creating good designs, you stand a better chance of avoiding the major pitfalls. Let's take a look at some of the important things to keep in mind during the design process. They may not make very much sense now, but it'll help to be aware of them as you read the rest of this chapter and start doing your own designs.

Be aware of the benefits of good design

Good design offers a number of benefits. Higher reliability, better maintainability, good code reuse, faster implementation, higher performance and lower resource requirements are all among the benefits available. Sometimes though, these attributes might be mutually exclusive (faster implementation may imply lower code reuse for example), so it pays to know which benefits you value the most.

Consider the *interface* separately from the implementation

The *interface* to a class is the way in which the set of functionality it offers to programmers is exposed and made available to them. In Smalltalk this is the set of methods which can be invoked by a programmer using the class, or inherited along with the instance variables by a subclass of the class. In order to maximise encapsulation, it is important that this interface (the 'protocol' the class understands in Smalltalk terms) is considered to be distinct from the *implementation* of the functionality. Implementation should be kept private to a class, in order that it may be modified and improved as the class programmer sees fit.

Try to hide complexity

This is another way of saying the same thing as above. If you can present a nice, simple, general interface to a class, and hide the complexity of how the class implements its functionality inside the class, do so. That way your classes will be easier to use, and you'll be at liberty to fiddle with implementation independently.

Minimise dependencies between classes

Modularity is greatly improved if classes are less knowledgeable about each other. This allows one class to be changed without affecting others. It is especially true that classes should not be knowledgeable of each other's implementation. Of course, sometimes you'll want to have communities of co-operating classes which are knowledgeable about each other. In this case you should consider the group of classes as if they were a 'module'. The classes in this module should then present a public interface which is distinct from the private protocol used between themselves.

Keep the user-interface separate from the application logic

Don't confuse this with the earlier guideline to keep a class's interface separate from its implementation. The separation of the user-interface from the application logic is a fundamental Smalltalk principle, again intended to optimise modularity. If you understand and adhere to the principles behind the MVC architecture you will almost automatically keep the user-interface separate from the application logic. It is all too easy to get them mixed up if you're not careful though, so if MVC isn't clear to you go back and have a look at chapters 8 and 9.

Factor-out complex algorithms

Just as in conventional programming, you should try to break complex algorithms into logical pieces. Not only will this make them easier to write, test and debug, but it may also provide pieces which can be reused independently. However, in view of the previous considerations, be careful about distributing an algorithm around different classes. This could make those classes too dependent on a knowledge of each other's implementation.

Factor-out complex variables

Don't try to 'encode' several aspects of an object's state in one variable. Doing so prejudices future development and reuse. Use one variable for each aspect of the state of an object.

Create as few special-purpose classes as possible

Remember that the fact that a single class can have many instances is a key way in which reuse is achieved in Smalltalk. If you're finding that you need to create a lot of special-purpose classes in your application, you probably need to think again about whether you've understood the general concepts you're trying to model.

Have a class road-map in mind

Remember that when you're designing for Smalltalk, you're not just designing for the Smalltalk language, what you're really doing is designing an extension to an existing (and very large) body of code—the class library. Try to make as much use of that body of code as you can. Even if you don't end up inheriting from anything other than `Object`, you'll still be designing classes which will live in that particular environment. Making your design compatible in form and function with the existing code will make things much easier when it comes to implementation. In other words, adopt the Smalltalk 'style' we're going to talk about in more detail in the next chapter.

Keep things simple

Obvious, but worth remembering. You'll find that by continuing to iterate over a design, it will get simpler and simpler, whilst the functionality it provides gets more general and hence more powerful.

Design Tasks

At the highest level, design is the process of going from an understanding of the desired behaviour of a system to a specification of the implementation of the system. If this were a purely mechanical process we could write a computer program to do it. Unfortunately (or fortunately for those whose job depends upon doing it), design requires a great deal of skill and judgement on the part of the designer.

Object-oriented design involves carrying out a number of tasks. Each task is highly dependent on decisions made during previous tasks. Decisions made during any task may also affect or change decisions made earlier. Thus, even design itself is an iterative process. However, we can break OOD down into a number of tasks which we can *consider* independently. Remember though that in reality these tasks may be merged, omitted, reordered, repeated or changed to suit the circumstances. Don't treat the following as a recipe to be followed slavishly—treat it as a list of ingredients. We'll look at a few of these tasks in more detail later on, and the list is summarised at the end of the chapter.

Decide on the required functionality

This task is very little different from its equivalent in conventional programming. The specification (which depending on circumstances, may be anything from a formal document to some ideas in your own head) will say *what* has to be achieved. This task is the first stage of determining *how* it will be achieved. What sort of data will you have to store? In what ways will you have to manipulate the data? What will the user-interface look like? In other words, how do requirements in the application domain map onto requirements in the computing domain?

There are many ways of extracting this kind of understanding, but one which works well is the use of 'scenarios'. Pick a particular aspect of the requirements and work through exactly what functionality will have to be provided to support that requirement. Do this for each important aspect of the requirements.

Identify which objects will provide the functionality

Once you know what functionality you're trying to provide, you can start to consider how it will be implemented. This task is the first of several aimed at 'finding the objects'. Objects can come from two places. They may be instances of existing classes, or they may be instances of classes written specially for this application.

Most of the existing classes you will use will come from the standard class library. Those that don't may have been written previously by you, or obtained from other people. You'll have to make sure these classes really will do the job you want them to, but if they do you'll be able to avoid many of the following tasks where these objects are concerned.

If you cannot find existing classes which implement the functionality you require, you will have to identify, design and implement them yourself. Identifying objects is the most tricky part of this process, and we'll deal with it in detail shortly.

Group the objects into classes

Whilst working out what new kinds of object your application will need, you'll almost inevitably be thinking in terms of classes. The only reason for talking about this task separately is to encourage you to iterate the process of looking for commonality amongst the different objects in your system. You should be asking questions like 'Are those two objects really instances of the same class?'

Decide how the objects will relate to each other

Objects relate to each other in several important ways. They hold references to each other, they send messages to each other and they inherit from each other. Leaving inheritance until later, what you need to do here is work out which objects know about which others, and what the message flows are between them.

In considering these relationships you will probably find it helpful to use diagrams of some sort. Use whatever kinds of diagram you feel comfortable with. You can use a standard notation if you like, or use one of your own. 'Object–relationship' diagrams, 'message exchange' diagrams, flowcharts and other types of diagram can all be used. Look back to Part I if you want to remind yourself of how diagrams of various types can be used to communicate information about structures of objects. Just draw whatever makes sense to you. Don't be bound by convention!

One thing to be very careful about when drawing object–relationship or similar diagrams is to distinguish between different kinds of relationship. This will especially apply later to *'contains'* or *'has a reference to'* as opposed to *'is an instance of'* and *'is a subclass of'*. Watch out, because it's very easy to end up talking at cross-purposes with someone you're discussing a design with.

Design the interfaces to the classes

Once you've decided what sorts of object you're going to implement, and how those objects will relate to each other, it should be a simple enough task to design the interfaces to the objects. This means deciding on what methods you will implement in which classes, what parameters they will take, what they will do (not how they're implemented) and what their return values will be. Try to keep the interface as *general* as possible.

Design the implementation of the classes

This means deciding on the required instance variables, and designing the methods which will implement the interfaces to the classes. We are deliberately considering this as a separate task from the design of the interface, in order to emphasise one of the design considerations introduced previously—keeping the interface separate from the implementation. However, this is really where design merges into coding in Smalltalk. If you have done a good job of specifying the interface and factoring-out complex operations, turning the functionality into working Smalltalk should be relatively easy.

Group the implementations using inheritance

Inheritance is the very last thing you should think about when designing classes in Smalltalk. This is because although it is very important and is a key factor in getting good reuse, you cannot really consider how your classes will inherit from each other until you know what they are going to do and how they are going to be implemented. Of course, as soon as you consider inheritance, you will want to go back and change details of the interface and implementation of your classes to make them more 'inheritable'. That's good, and is just a part of the iterative process of design.

You must resist the temptation to get caught up in thinking about inheritance too early in the design process. It's much better to leave it until later, at least until you have a lot of experience and can 'look ahead' easily. In keeping with this spirit, inheritance is the last thing we shall consider in detail in this chapter.

Identifying the Objects

This is really the crux of OOD, and for most people it is by far the most difficult part of working in Smalltalk. The good news is that it *is* something that becomes natural after a while. In the meantime, let's look at a few guidelines.

You know by now that everything in Smalltalk is an object. But remember that lots of different things *can* be objects. If you want examples of the kinds of things which it makes sense to model as Smalltalk objects you've only got to spend some time browsing the system class library. One rule-of-thumb is that if you can talk about it, and it's important to your system, it should probably be an object. However, try to stick to a one object = one idea rule. Don't overload a single object with multiple meanings. If there's lots of behaviour in a class which isn't relevant to every user of that class, you should probably consider moving it.

It's easy to conceive of objects which model 'real world' entities. If you're dealing with people, places and things in your program you will probably think of having objects which represent those people, places and things. Objects can also model 'computer world' entities. If your program needs to open files or windows then it's pretty obvious you'll need objects which represent files and windows. What is not so obvious is that objects can also be used to model *processes*.

Processes include tasks, activities, operations, commands and all the other non-physical things your program has to deal with. For example, you might model an electronic equipment test procedure in a class. Doing so would allow you to create instances of the class whenever equipment tests were initiated. These instances would not only be knowledgeable about the sequencing of the test, but also about the state of the individual test they represented. Similarly, you could represent the process of opening a bank account using a class. Instances of this class would be responsible for knowing which actions must be completed to open the account, and would hold the results of performing each of those actions.

Modelling processes as objects instead of just embedding process-related code in 'physical' objects has a number of important advantages. It means that you are able to use inheritance to specialise and reuse code along process lines, as well as along physical-modelling lines. It also means that you can have several processes (not actual computer processes, but processes being modelled) in a state of partial completion, with the state of each concurrently executing process being explicitly held in an object instead of being implicitly represented in the call-stack.

It helps to think about some of the characteristics of the objects you might use in your program. Which 'layer' of your system (if your architecture is structured that way) will they be in? Will they be long-lived (such as a person's bank account) or temporary (such as a single transaction)? Will they be active (such as test object driving a sequence of actions) or passive (a test log responding only to requests to store or retrieve information)? Will they be general-purpose (an interface to a database), or special-purpose (a new kind of widget)? Will they represent a physical entity (like a person) or a conceptual entity (like a credit record)? Will they be private (doing a job just for you in a particular part of the system) or public (used all over the system)? Finally, will they represent the whole of something (such as a book) or just a part of something (such as a page)?

This last point is an important one. It is a good idea to try to break things down as much as possible and use separate objects to represent the pieces. Then you can use other objects to aggregate these pieces together into coherent collections. Designing things this way will give smaller, simpler classes which are easier to reuse and easier to modify. It'll also make it easier to deal with inheritance later. For example, if you need to create an object which models a simple appointment list, you might think of making it contain two collections—one containing strings representing the appointment description and the other containing integers representing the appointment time. A much better thing to do would be to create a class which models the idea of a single appointment. Instances of this class would hold a single string and a single integer. Then the appointment list would just be a collection of these appointment objects.

Relationships Between Objects

As we've observed, relationships between objects can be of several kinds. Some of these relationships are what you might call peer-to-peer, and others are distinctly directional. Amongst the directional ones are the relationship between an instance and its class (in Smalltalk this is just as much a relationship between objects as any other), and the inheritance relationship between classes (also definitely a relationship between objects, since classes like everything else in Smalltalk are objects).

Neglecting these special kinds of relationship, let's briefly consider the other kinds of non-inheritance relationship you might create in your design, and look at how they map into Smalltalk implementations.

Associations

You may create situations in your design where objects have to know about each other because they are *associated* in some way. Usually, but not always, these will be one-to-one relationships. They are typically implemented by creating an instance variable in one object which will contain the other object. The diagram below illustrates the idea. Your only real consideration is whether to make them two-way (both objects

Associations between objects (implemented using instance variables) can be two-way (customer/creditRecord) or one-way (customer/address).

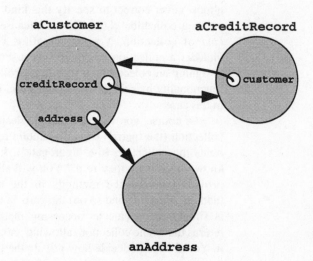

know about each other) or one-way (only one object knows about the other). This is a matter of style as well as necessity. If you don't need the two-way association, its up to you whether you create it in case you or a reuser of your code needs it in the future. If you make two-way associations you may wish to specify convenience methods which use the accessing methods to set the values of the instance variables in both objects at the same time to ensure they remain consistent.

Aggregations

Aggregations occur when you have got an object which represents the sum of its parts. This may be an object which simply has a number of associations with other objects, each implemented by a single instance variable. For example, a car has an engine, a transmission, a body and so on. Again you'll have to decide whether to maintain one- or two-way pointers, but otherwise this is straight forward.

The only thing to watch out for here is not to fall into the trap of trying to use inheritance to represent this relationship. Just say to yourself 'an engine is not a kind of car'. Part/whole relationships actually bring about another sort of hierarchy within your program (in addition to inheritance) which you yourself are responsible for implementing. This hierarchy may be several levels deep, and in fact there may be more than one such hierarchy.

An aggregation may also be an object which is holding a *collection* of other objects. For example a book includes a collection of pages. It is almost never correct to specify this kind of object as a subclass of an existing collection class. This is because you are not creating a new *kind* of collection. You are creating a new kind of object which *includes* a collection of other objects. Encapsulating functionality by designing an object which includes a collection, rather than inheriting functionality by subclassing a collection, is the preferred form of reuse in this case.

Of course, you will still have to decide whether the objects in the collection (the 'parts') should maintain references to the object which holds the collection (the 'aggregate'). In other words, do the pages know which book they're in? You will also have to decide whether to provide convenience methods in the aggregate for manipulating (adding, removing and so on) the parts in the collection. The alternative is simply to provide an accessing method in the aggregate which returns the whole collection, allowing another object complete access to it. You'll have to decide how private the fact that you're implementing the aggregation as a collection really is.

Dependency

This is really a special case of association. It occurs when one object is interested in *changes* to another. Smalltalk provides a special mechanism called 'the dependency mechanism' specifically for dealing with this kind of relationship. It is the foundation of MVC and so if your design incorporates user-interface elements you will need to consider carefully where you are creating dependency relationships. However, you can create dependencies between other (non-UI) objects if you wish. This is a powerful facility, but be careful when specifying it, because dependency relationships are more difficult to debug than explicit associations. This is because it is simply less obvious if two objects are communicating via dependency.

Designing for Reuse

One of the big promises of OOP is the possibility of being able to reuse code from previous applications. Unfortunately, like so many other things this reusability does not come for free and neither is it automatic. It is a fact that classes must be *designed* to be reused if they are to be reusable. Before looking at designing for reuse though, let's consider what we mean by 'reusable'.

What is reusability?

Classes are only reusable if other programmers are more inclined to use them than to write their own. This means that a supposedly reusable class must not only meet the technical needs of the application but must also be easy to use and *understandable*. Meeting the technical needs means performing the task required reliably, efficiently and without unnecessary side-effects. Making a class easy to use and understandable means making sure that what it does is predictable, which in turn generally means following the Smalltalk 'style' discussed in the next chapter.

It's important to remember that not all classes *have* to be reusable. Reusability costs time and effort, and those resources should be spent on making the most appropriate classes reusable. Just as reusability is not automatic with OOP, it is not a given that every class must be written to be reusable. However, if you've decided that a class *is* to be made reusable, you must decide in what *way* it is to be reused.

Kinds of reusability

There are two interfaces to a class as far as reuse is concerned. A reuser may *encapsulate* the class (placing an instance of it inside an instance of their own class), or they may *inherit* from it. These two mechanisms reflect two models of reuse, both of which are available in Smalltalk. You can think of a class library as a collection of parts which can be plugged together, or you can think of a class library as a tree which can be inherited from at various points. In Smalltalk it is usually the case that *parts* are more reusable than *subclasses*.

If you've been doing any programming in Smalltalk you'll realise how much more frequently you make instances of the existing classes than you inherit from them. You make instances of numbers, strings, collections, widgets and so on all the time. It is very rare that you inherit from any of these classes. **Object** is by far the most common superclass. What this means is that when you create your reusable classes you should think harder about how someone else will use *instances* of them than about how they might *inherit* from them. Designing for inheritance is hard enough when you're going to be the inheritor. Trying to design for unknown inheritance in the future is too hard to be of common use.

Building parts designed to be plugged together (the technical word for this plugging is *composition*) also allows you to bypass the limitations of the single-inheritance system Smalltalk uses (each class has exactly one superclass, instead of being a combination of many parent classes). Each part of a composite object can have its own place in its own inheritance hierarchy. The location of a single monolithic equivalent in the class hierarchy would always have to be a compromise.

You must also decide to what *extent* you want a class to be reusable. If you've created a class which you will use in more than one place in an application, you have in effect written a reusable class. However, you might want to go further and make the class reusable by others in your team working on the same application. You might want the class to be reusable by you or others in your team in future applications (a very common form of reuse is using a class you wrote for a previous project in your current project—you have no learning curve for the class, you presumably trust it, and so are motivated to reuse it). Finally, you might be trying to create a class which is reusable by someone you've never met, who might even pay money for it. The extent to which you want a class to be reusable will affect how much effort you put into the following considerations for reuse.

Writing reusable code

The most obvious thing is to try to make your code generic. A key enabler for this in Smalltalk is its 'typelessness'. If you don't need to restrict the type of an object in the interface to a class, don't. If you do, only restrict it as far as necessary. For example, when a method accepts a collection as a parameter, make your code work with as many different kinds of collection as possible, rather than just say arrays.

One way to make a class more general is to avoid hard-coding constants into methods. Bring them out into the interface as parameters to methods, if that makes sense. Of course, doing this may complicate the interface to the class, so a common ploy is to create simpler versions of various methods (called *convenience* methods). These take fewer parameters than the complex methods, but don't reimplement them. They simply call the more complex methods with default values for the parameters. You can see this happening frequently in the class library, where it sometimes goes through many levels of increasing generality (and increasing numbers of parameters) before the method which actually does the work is called.

Possibly in conflict with the above (but then that's where your judgement comes in), is the desire to *encapsulate* as much of the implementation of the class as possible. In other words, don't expose through the interface features which are internal to the way the class works, and which don't need to be accessed to alter or configure the service it provides.

Try to design your classes so that users only need to know about features they actually use. Providing convenience methods is a good way of doing this. Also, aim to make your classes 'combinable' and pluggable, in the way that the adaptors we looked at in Part I are.

In general, just try to think about what future uses your class may be put to. You will never be able to predict every possible future use, and unless your class has the highest reusability requirements, you shouldn't waste your time trying to do so. But, if you can find a way to achieve the immediate purpose of the class, whilst also designing the functionality in a general way, it's probably worth choosing that way.

Using Inheritance

After 'finding the objects', making use of inheritance is probably the thing newcomers to object-oriented programming find they have most difficulty with. In fact, even experienced programmers tie themselves in knots with it occasionally, but thankfully it is also something which gets easier to do as time goes by. The important thing to remember is that inheritance is a facility intended to make things *easier*, not more difficult. You don't have to struggle to create an incredibly deep and efficient inheritance hierarchy if that simply isn't possible. However, if you know a few simple things about how to use inheritance (and how not to use it) you'll find it can make your code simpler and more elegant.

We're going to assume here that you understand how inheritance in Smalltalk works. That's not to say that you have to know how it is implemented by the Smalltalk system, just that you need to understand that methods and variables are inherited from a superclass by a subclass, that you can over-ride inherited methods and so on. If you're unsure what is meant by inheritance in Smalltalk, take another look at Chapter 2—*An Introduction to Objects*.

Don't worry about it too early

The first rule of inheritance is to leave it until later. Don't try to think about it too early. You should at least know what the various classes in your design are going to do before you can even think about how they are (or could be *redesigned* to be) similar in their implementations. Sometimes you will even have coded a working system before you go back and start making use of inheritance. Sometimes it can take practical experience of using the classes you've built before you realise the full generality of what they're actually doing are able to factor-out some of that functionality into a superclass. In doing this be aware that the process of creating an inheritance hierarchy can be a top-down, bottom-up, or even middle-out activity.

Use inheritance to reuse code

The second rule is to use inheritance for code reuse and nothing else. Remember that you can read the inheritance relationship between a subclass and its superclass as '*is a kind of*'. But 'is a kind of' can be interpreted in a number of ways. There's the human-speak 'is a kind of', and there's the computer-speak 'is a kind of' for example. You must distinguish between the kind of thing something is in real life, and the kind of thing the object used to model it in Smalltalk is. Thus, a trout may be a kind of fish in human-speak, but a kind of **ApplicationModel** in Smalltalk, if an **ApplicationModel** with a few additions is good for modelling trout.

It is very easy to fall into the trap of using the inheritance hierarchy as a classification scheme for the real objects you're trying to model, instead of using it for optimising code reuse in the Smalltalk objects you're modelling them with. This is really the difference between sub-*typing* and sub-*classing*. A good example of correct use of inheritance in the system class library is the class **Process**, which is actually a subclass of the class **Link**. In real life, a process is a kind of course of action, but in Smalltalk its important features share a lot in common with **Link** and so it is modelled as a special kind of **Link**.

Another good example of the difference between a *conceptual* hierarchy (in the real world) and an *implementation* hierarchy (in the Smalltalk world) is the difference between a circle and an ellipse. In the real world, a circle is a special kind of ellipse in which the major and minor axes are of equal length. So circle is a subtype of ellipse. However in the Smalltalk world we'd probably make **circle** the superclass with a single **diameter** variable, and subclass it to get **Ellipse** which would add an extra variable.

As a reminder, you should also avoid trying to use inheritance to create a 'part-of' hierarchy. It sounds stupid, but it's remarkably easy to think that way, at least until you're very comfortable with using inheritance. A door is not a kind of house, even though it is part of it. Use another relationship, like an association (see earlier). Remember that inheritance is only one of many types of relationships between objects which you have at your disposal.

Use inheritance to specialise behaviour

If you think about it, you'll see that Smalltalk's inheritance mechanism may be used to get a subclass to add, modify or delete behaviour from the superclass (see diagram on the next page). Adding is achieved simply by defining more methods, or by redefining (over-riding) a particular method and putting in a call to **super** . Modifying behaviour is achieved by over-riding a method to do something different, thus *replacing* the inherited original functionality. Deleting behaviour can be achieved in Smalltalk by over-riding a method with one which contains simply the expression **self shouldNotImplement** . This will raise an exception if anyone tries to send that message to your object.

Inheritance in Smalltalk is almost always *additive*. That is, additional methods are put in a subclass to increase the functionality of the subclass over that of the superclass, or methods are over-ridden to enhance or modify their behaviour. *Subtractive* inheritance is rarely

Inheritance can be used to leave functionality alone (method A), modify it (B) replace it (C), remove it(D), or add it (E).

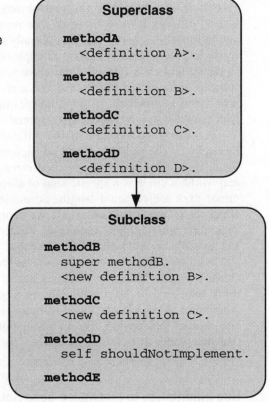

used. This means that subclasses tend to be more specific versions of their superclasses. This is because it is awkward to take a class which models some concept and make it model a more general concept by subclassing it. Look out for this when you design your inheritance hierarchies. Start with the most general model at the top, and proceed to the more specific lower down.

You can also think of this as meaning that subclassing restricts the set of things which an instance of the class could represent. For example, the **Collection** class in Smalltalk represents the concept of any kind of collection of objects. However, one of it's subclasses, **SequenceableCollection**, has already restricted the set of things which it may be used to model to collections of objects which have a well defined order. A subclass of that class (**ArrayedCollection**) restricts that ordering to one which is defined by external integer keys, and so it continues on down the class hierarchy.

The only time an exception to this rule should occur is when you want to make a system class do more general things than it does. It is much easier to subclass a system class than to 'superclass' it. You *can* attempt to insert a class halfway down an existing hierarchy, but you had better watch that you don't alter any of the behaviour of the lower classes by doing so. So you're stuck with trying to take a specific implementation and make it more general in a subclass.

Use inheritance to share behaviour

Earlier in this book we looked at *abstract* superclasses. These are classes of which no instances are ever made. Abstract superclasses can be used to collect together functionality which is shared amongst several *concrete* subclasses, but which isn't complete in itself. This solves a problem which sometimes occurs when you want to create two classes which share functionality, but you find that neither is a natural superclass of the other. Simply 'abstract' the shared functionality into a third class, and make the two classes concrete subclasses of this third class, as in the diagram below. This allows the two classes to be siblings—sharing common functionality from the superclass. A design which is structured in this way is much more elegant than it would be if you forced a class to a be subclass of another class when that wasn't really 'logical'.

Inheritance can be used to share functionality by defining common methods in an abstract superclass and unique methods in concrete subclasses.

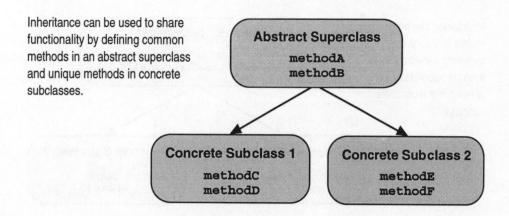

137

Watch out for inappropriate sharing of functionality through inheritance though. If a class is inheriting a whole load of methods which simply are not applicable to its purpose then they should probably be removed from its superclass, and moved to a sibling class. Either that, or the whole hierarchy needs restructuring. For some good examples of how to structure an abstract superclass hierarchy, browse the **Collection** class and some of its subclasses (the class comment will usually tell you whether the class is intended to be abstract or concrete).

Use inheritance to realise behaviour

Another reason to create abstract superclasses is to provide a *specification* of an interface which is then *implemented* in one or more subclasses. Remember that this separation of interface from implementation is one of the goals of good OOD.

In Smalltalk, a method can be specified but left unimplemented in a superclass by writing a method with the correct name and parameters, and then implementing it using just the expression **self subclassResponsibility**. The method is then over-ridden in the subclass with a proper implementation, as in the diagram below. This kind of construction will cause an exception if a message invoking that method is sent to an instance of the superclass or to an instance of a subclass which has failed to over-ride the method. Both the method and the exception are a signal to the subclasser that they need to reimplement the method.

Inheritance can be used to realise functionality by declaring a method in an abstract superclass and defining it in a concrete subclass.

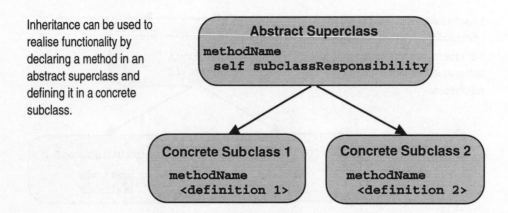

When defining an interface to a method in a superclass which is then implemented in a subclass, you can still invoke the not-yet-implemented method in other superclass code. For example, in the class **Magnitude** the < method is defined but not implemented. However, it is then used to implement the > method, also in **Magnitude**. This is fine because a concrete subclass of **Magnitude** will implement its own < which means that the inherited > will call that method and consequently work properly. Take a look at the system class hierarchy in this area if this isn't clear, and for other examples try using the **browse—>senders** command from the launcher to see every class and method which uses **subclassResponsibility**.

Summary

Throughout this chapter we have looked at a variety of the important principles of object-oriented design as it applies to Smalltalk. We started by looking at design considerations. The important design considerations were:

- Consider the interface separately from the implementation.
- Try to hide complexity.
- Minimise dependencies between classes.
- Keep the user-interface separate from the application logic.
- Factor-out complex algorithms.
- Factor-out complex variables.
- Create as few special-purpose classes as possible.
- Have a class road-map in mind.
- Keep things simple.

We also looked at the tasks typically undertaken by developers when designing Smalltalk programs. Design is an iterative and opportunistic activity, so these tasks may be re–ordered, some of them may be omitted, and some of them repeated as your understanding of whatever you're designing improves. The tasks we looked at were:

- Deciding on the required functionality.
- Identifying which objects will provide the functionality.
- Grouping the objects into classes.
- Deciding how the objects will relate to each other.
- Designing the interfaces to the classes.
- Designing the implementation of the classes
- Grouping the implementations using inheritance.

Finally, we looked in more detail at *identifying* the objects, understanding the *relationships* between them (associations, aggregations, dependency), designing for good reusability and lastly at how to use inheritance effectively.

That's all there is to it. If you were looking to this chapter for a magic spell to help you 'find the objects' for your application then you will have been disappointed. However, if you manage to keep in mind just some of the guidelines we've discussed, and you remember to refer back to here when you come across the circumstances we've considered, you'll find that designing Smalltalk systems soon ceases to be a difficult task and becomes an easy and natural precursor to coding in Smalltalk. The art of *coding* in Smalltalk is therefore the subject of the next chapter.

Appendix: Design Methodologies

Hewlett Packard's *Fusion* methodology for object-oriented projects was developed at HP Labs Bristol. It is fully described in:

> *Object Oriented Development: The Fusion Method*
> Derek Coleman *et al.*, Prentice-Hall 1994
> ISBN 0-13-338823-9

ParcPlace's *Object Behavior Analysis and Design* (OBA/D) for *VisualWorks* projects is described in:

> *Succeeding with Objects: Decision Frameworks for Project Mgt.*
> Adele Goldberg and Kenneth S. Rubin, Addison-Wesley 1995
> ISBN 0-201-62878-3

Coding in Smalltalk

In the preceding chapter we looked at a number of aspects of designing for Smalltalk. The advice and techniques we discussed there were optimised for, and presented in the context of Smalltalk. Even so, we didn't get quite as far as discussing specific coding techniques. In this chapter we'll attempt to redress the balance by talking about coding in Smalltalk.

Throughout this chapter we'll consider a number of different aspects of Smalltalk coding style. First we'll cover the common naming conventions which help make Smalltalk source-code more readable. We'll then look at ways of accessing instance variables and constants which promote better reusability. Next we'll consider some general coding advice, how to structure methods and so on. Then we'll cover the best ways to use comments, and finish with a discussion about writing efficient code.

Smalltalk with Style

As you should have realised by now, the act of programming in Smalltalk is really the act of extending a body of code (the standard class library) to make it do the things *you* want it to do. The standard class library has developed over many years (many more than you might think in fact—Smalltalk has been around since 1972!). Over all that time specific ways of using the Smalltalk language have evolved. You might almost say that there is a common Smalltalk 'idiom'.

This Smalltalk idiom is a particular way of using the language to express programming ideas. It is shared by most of the code in the class library. Even though the class library has been developed by many people, the style is remarkably consistent throughout. This is extremely useful since it helps you do that most important thing in Smalltalk—work out what a class or method does just by reading the source-code. It also provides you with ready-made ways of expressing certain programming constructions—constructions which are robust, easy to understand and easy to modify and maintain.

Occasionally though, you will come across examples of different ways of expressing ideas. This is often confusing enough to illustrate the value of consistency in the use of Smalltalk. If you adopt the standard style of usage, your code will fit in better with the code in the class library it is extending. It will also be more readable and more easily understood by other Smalltalk programmers. It may even be more reusable.

Naming Conventions

Smalltalk has very few rules about naming classes, variables, methods, categories and protocols. The few that do exist were quickly covered in Chapter 4—*The Smalltalk Language*. Our interest here is in the *conventions* which govern the way Smalltalk programmers name their classes, variables and other entities. These conventions have evolved over time to make Smalltalk code read in a particular, almost English-like way.

Variables

To begin with, you should always follow the rule (even though it's not completely enforced by the system) that global variables, pool variables and class variables all start with a capital letter, whilst instance and temporary variables start with a lower-case letter. After that, try to make your variable names as descriptive as possible.

Remember that variable names can be as long as you like. You might want to try to include something about the function of the variable, as well as the type of object it is expected to contain. For example, **occupiedRectangle**, **labelText**, **examResults**. The last example uses a common convention to indicate a collection—it's a plural—a collection of **examResult** objects.

If you want to name a variable which holds a boolean state, use something like **isBig, wasConverted, hasBeenEdited**. Using these kinds of name allows you to write classic Smalltalk expressions such as:

```
occupiedRectangle hasBeenEdited ifTrue:
                    ["Do Something"].
```

In this case, **hasBeenEdited** is the accessing method for the instance variable called **hasBeenEdited** in some class of which the object **occupiedRectangle** is an instance.

Parameters

A common convention for naming parameters in method definitions is to use the name of the class of the object you expect to be passed, prefixed with '**a**' or '**an**' as is appropriate. For example, **anOrderedCollection**, **aDictionary**, **aString**. If a parameter in your method could be an instance of several different classes, use the lowest common superclass. For example, **aCollection**, or in the extreme, **anObject**. The latter is not as meaningless as it may seem *if* it is communicating the fact that an object of *any* class may be passed as a parameter.

Method Names

Just like variable names, you should try to make method names (or selectors as they are technically known) descriptive of their purpose. There is no limit on length, so again you should use as long a name as you need (within reason of course). Browsing the class hierarchy will show you that there are some very long method names indeed out there!

Methods whose only purpose is to access variables should be named after the variable they access. For example, if you have an instance variable called **size**, the method which returns its value should be called **size**, and not **returnSize**, **getSize**, **giveSize** or anything else. Similarly, the method which sets its value should be called **size:**, not **setSize:** or anything like that.

In a similar vein, try also to make method names *declarative* rather than *imperative*. In other words, it is better to use **totalArea** than **computeTotalArea**. This makes the method name communicate the kind of value it *returns*. This is important when you want to cascade messages. Compare the following two expressions:

```
CricketPitch area asSquareMetres.
CricketPitch giveArea convertToSquareMetres.
```

At the moment it may seem a subtle distinction, but the first expression reads much more clearly to Smalltalk programmers than the second. If you really want to use words like 'convert', use the past participle instead—**convertedToSquareMetres**.

When naming a method which takes several parameters, try to create a name which conveys the purpose and if possible the type of each parameter. For example:

```
PaintBox drawLineFrom: x to: y
            usingPen: aPen inColour: #red.
```

Note that in this case, we broke the rule about making method names declarative (**drawLineFrom**... instead of **lineFrom**...). This is because we are interested in the *side-effect* (the line getting drawn) and not the return-value of the method.

Finally when naming a method, think of the service it provides, not the way it provides it. In other words name the method after the *interface* not after the *implementation*. Doing this will avoid revealing things about the way your implementation works by the way you name your methods.

Classes

Remember that class names are really global variables, and so you should follow the same rule that they start with a capital letter. Just as before, the real intent should be to communicate the purpose of the class. However, you may also wish to communicate something about the class hierarchy, if that is important. For example **OrderedCollection** is a subclass of **Collection**. You might go on to create a subclass called **OptimizedOrderedCollection** (just as an example). This naming convention is not always necessary or desirable though—it's a matter of judgement. For example, **Set** is also a subclass of **Collection**, but in this case the word 'Set' communicates more about the purpose of the class than any more contrived name ever could.

Avoid the temptation to prefix class names with your initials, the project name or your company name. Although it might seem that this would make them easier to separate from the system classes, it actually just makes them difficult to distinguish from *each other*. You should be aiming to integrate your classes into the system anyway.

Categories and Protocols

Categories and protocols exist to help *you* organise your classes and methods. Use names which facilitate this. Remember you can include space characters. Some people like to use prefixes which indicate who the classes in a category were written by. This is acceptable in category names, since they don't appear in your code. Others like to indicate which project the category was written for. The categories in the class library generally use a two-level naming scheme, and it's worth considering whether to adopt this for your project. For example, **Server-Views** or **Framework-Datastore**.

We looked previously at the 'standard' protocol names which the classes in the system library use. Names like **accessing**, **updating**, **displaying** and **private** are absolutely fundamental to the Smalltalk idiom. If you use *any* of the naming conventions discussed here, use this one. It is possibly one of the biggest contributing factors to making your code readable by others. However, not only should you *use* the names, you should use them properly. Don't put anything other than methods which provide access to instance variables in **accessing** for example. If a method is private (to be used only by you) put it in the **private** protocol. When you need to create new protocol names, try to name them with the task of either you or someone else trying to understand your code in mind. A good guideline to follow is to use present participles as protocol names—words which end in '-ing'. For example, **calculating** or **printing**.

Accessing Instance Variables

A matter of style which is sometimes hotly debated among Smalltalkers concerns the accessing of instance variables. If a class defines or inherits instance variables, those variables can be accessed in the methods defined on the class simply by naming the variable. This applies both for assigning values to the variable, and using the variable's value in expressions. For example, the following expression is legal within a method of a class which has instance variables called **area**, **width** and **height**:

```
area := width * height.
```

Typically, a programmer will also define **accessing** methods, which permit other objects to access the variables by sending a message. In this case the instance variables above could be accessed from outside their own object using expressions like:

```
MyObject area.
MyObject width: 25.
```

It is often suggested however, that an object should also access its *own* instance variables by sending messages to itself, and not by directly naming them. In this case, the earlier method fragment would perhaps become something like this (with parentheses added for clarity):

```
self area: (self width) * (self height).
```

Provided the methods **area:**, **width** and **height** are defined correctly (to do nothing more than access the variables), this expression has exactly the same effect as the first one. So why would anyone want to do this? The answer is that by avoiding direct access to instance variables, you can potentially increase flexibility and as a result enhance reusability. But how?

Instance variables really represent properties of an object. Specifically, they are properties whose actual values are held (or cached) in the object, rather than being computed as required. However, what starts life as an instance variable, may later need to become a computed value. Now if that instance variable is only accessed via a method, this becomes a simple task of replacing the accessing method with one of the same name which computes the value in some arbitrarily complex way instead of simply returning it. If the variable has been accessed by naming it directly, the situation is more complicated. A new method must be created, and every single reference to the variable throughout the class and all its subclasses must be changed to messages invoking the new method.

This process gets especially complicated and messy if the variable is defined in a superclass, and you want to make it a computed value in a subclass. Unless you go and modify the superclass (which might not be allowed), you have to over-ride in your subclass *all* the methods of the superclass which access the variable, replacing all references to the variable with a message expression. If the original writer of the superclass had used accessing messages in the first place, you'd only have to over-ride the *accessing* methods in your subclass.

Looking back at the above example, we can imagine that there is an instance variable called **area**. We might define an accessing method which simply returns the value of the **area** variable:

```
area
    ^area.
```

Now, provided we use it consistently in all the rest of our code, then when we later want (either in a subclass, or a later version of the same class) to replace the notion of 'area' with a computed value instead of a cached one, we simply redefine the method **area**, perhaps as follows:

```
area
    ^(width * height).
```

Now it doesn't matter how many references there are to **area**. Because they are message expressions and not variable references they will automatically access the new computed value. What's more, if the change from a variable to a computed value did happen in a subclass, then because of the way method lookup works, references to **area** in instances of the superclass would continue to invoke the old method (returning the value of the instance variable), whilst instances of the subclass would invoke the new method (returning the computed value).

So much for the claimed benefits of accessing instance variables only through messages. What are the disadvantages? The most obvious disadvantage is performance. Accessing your own instance variables via a message is necessarily slower than directly referencing them. The accessing message does exactly the same variable reference as you would have done, to which the time for a message pass must be added.

It is up to you to decide whether this has any impact at all on the performance of your code, and if so whether that impact is a price worth paying for the advantages we've just discussed. You could use the profiler provided as part of the *VisualWorks Advanced Programming ObjectKit* to decide which variables to refer to directly and which to use accessing methods for. You might also be able to improve your use of accessing messages (for example by caching a value in a temporary variable inside a loop instead of accessing it repeatedly).

Variable accesses via message expressions are also less readable than direct references. But in a sense, that's part of the point. The idea is to isolate the *user* of a value from the *implementation* of that value as an instance variable or a computed value. Again, it's a matter of judgement and personal opinion as to whether clarity of code, or encapsulation is most important.

Finally, having to define accessing methods even for supposedly 'private' variables (variables which you don't intend to be accessed from outside instances of the class they're defined or inherited in) may make you uncomfortable. Remember though that nothing is really private in Smalltalk. All you can do is flag your intentions by naming a protocol correctly (for example **private-accessing**). Ultimately, someone else could always define their own accessing method on your class, or use the **instVarAt:** method defined on **Object**. (Have a browse to see what this method does, but never use it unless you want to be branded as a 'hacker'!)

147

Accessing Constants

Remember that all of the above applies equally to class variables, global variables and constants. A very good example is the use of a method to define and access a class which is somehow linked to another class. This occurs in very many **View** subclasses, which implement the method **defaultControllerClass** to return the class of the controller which should normally be used with the view (which incidentally, is why controllers appear to hide in the background of the MVC triads). This gives a single place where the class may be changed, rather than all sorts of direct references to the controller class hidden in the view class. Browse the implementors of **default*** to see lots of examples of this kind of usage.

Just as in conventional programming, if there is some other fundamental constant which is important to a class you're writing, put it in a method and access it that way, rather than hard-coding it into your methods all over the place. You could for example, define a method such as:

```
minimumSize
    ^25@100.
```

and then access the **minimumSize** constant when required by doing:

```
self minimumSize.
```

Structuring Methods

One of the main things you should do when writing methods in a class is to try to keep them small. Anything much more than ten lines is probably getting too big (the average in the standard class library is around seven). Try to factor out the functionality of a long method into two or more methods. Just like using temporary variables to hold intermediate results, this will make your code easier to read, easier to modify and not much more inefficient. Make these methods as general-purpose as possible, and then 'compose up' the functionality you actually require in the main methods. That way, you'll give yourself a lot more flexibility when it comes to modifying your code.

Try also to format your code in a consistent way. Some people use the built-in formatter (**format** on the *operate* menu in any code pane). Others dislike the format it generates (although in theory you could change it!). Either way, a consistent format will make your code easier

and everything else. Feel free to put in extra
ou want to, assuming it makes your code more
ou. Be aware though that the formatter (if you
it again!

cally return **self** if nothing else is explicitly
the fact that your method returns **self** is an
s design, you might want to consider making it
This is also what you should return (rather than
a point in a method where you want to return,
but the return value. That allows you to cascade
ects, instead of getting the next message in a
hich is virtually guaranteed not to understand it).
t to use a conditional expression (**ifTrue:**,
to think about whether you could get the same
your methods to send a message to a different
ds, let the method lookup mechanism and its
ive you the same result. This is especially true if
ing the *class* of an object before deciding what to
sign that your design is not structured quite right.
cceptable to test an object's *functionality*, rather
example, you might define a method called
head in several classes. The method would return
ending on whether that particular class implements
tever that might be). Then you could use an

```
ementsLookAhead
"do one thing"]
["do another thing"].
```

that the choice of what to do is being made
e class of the object. This gives you the freedom to
modify the way the choice works, without having to modify the class
structure. (If you get really desperate you can actually test whether a
particular object will understand a message by using the **respondsTo:**
method defined on class **Object**. This is not to be recommended
though, except for the most ardent hacker).

Finally, just as in all programming languages, you should make
sure you initialise all variables before using them. Although they get
initialised to **nil** by the system, if you actually want them to have that
value, it's clearer to a reader to put in an assignment statement
explicitly making that happen.

Other Coding Guidelines

Having looked at Smalltalk naming conventions, how to access variables and constants and how to structure methods in Smalltalk, we'll consider a collection of other coding guidelines. All of these come under the category of common sense. This means that whilst they are generally useful, there will always be specific circumstances in which you'll want to do something different.

Variables with Discrete States

Always use **false** and **true** if you are dealing with a boolean state, and not **0** and **1**, or **nil** and some non-**nil** object. Tests for these values are optimised by the compiler (which by the way means that their definitions are one of the few pieces of code you can't alter). It also makes your code say directly what you want, especially if you name your variables appropriately (**isCooked**, **wasRaw**, etc.)

If you have a need for a variable which takes a fixed number of values, try to use a symbol (not a string—symbols are more efficient since they are unique and can be compared with ==) rather than say a number to encode this value. For example use **#large**, **#medium** and **#small**, to *describe* something's size rather than **3**, **2** and **1** to *encode* it. In the following three expressions, consider how much easier it is to understand what the second is doing than the first. The third expression is easier still and becomes available if you write a method called **isLarge** which encapsulates the **size = #large** test and returns either **true** or **false**.

```
MyObject size = 3 ifTrue: ["do something"].
MyObject size = #large ifTrue: ["do something"].
MyObject isLarge ifTrue: ["do something"].
```

Using Dictionaries

Dictionaries are one of the most useful building blocks in the standard class library. It's easy to conceive of using them as a simple data structure to hold pairs of objects, organised as 'name', and 'object'. But remember that dictionaries can hold *any* kind of object. This makes much more complex and powerful uses possible. For example, a dictionary may be used as a kind of control structure by putting blocks in as the values, and some other objects as the keys. This allows a kind of 'case' statement to be constructed if you wish. The first expression below shows a dictionary being initialised in this way (which need only happen once), and the second expression shows the way in which it might be used:

```
MyDict    at: #Small put: ["do a small thing"];
          at: #Medium put: ["do a medium thing"];
          at: #Large put: ["do a large thing"].

(MyDict at: case) value.
```

Managing Unique Objects

Sometimes you might think you'll only ever need one object of a particular type in a program. For example, you might need an object whose job it is to manage some kind of unique resource—the filesystem, a central look-up table, or perhaps an external interface. In these circumstances it is very tempting to make this object a class. In other words, it seems logical to create a special class and write class methods which do the work of this object, especially if the object really needs a unique name which is well known throughout the system (just like a classname).

This way of creating such an object is not the best however. A much better approach is to create the class, and create a single instance of it to do the work. The main reason for this is that you can never really be sure that you (or someone else) won't one day want to make *more than one* instance of this apparently unique object. It also means that your unique object inherits only the functionality of instances, and not the inappropriate functionality of classes. Remember that inheriting *only* the appropriate functionality is one of the guidelines you should use when designing classes.

In practice, the standard way to deal with this situation is to create the class and give it a class variable called **Default**. Then create a class method called **initialize** which initialises this variable to hold the required single instance of the class. Finally, create a class method called **default**, which returns the value of the class variable **Default**. Then, when the rest of your code wants to use this object it can refer to it using the expression **MyClassName default**. Now if you or anyone else wants to create more instances of the class you are free to do so. You may or may not then want to create additional class variables to hold these instances. To find examples of classes which use this way of structuring code use the **Browse—>implementors of...** command from the launcher to browse the implementors of **default**.

151

Unwinding Actions

Sometimes it is important to undo actions you have taken, especially if an exception occurs. The classic example is closing a file which has been opened, but in Smalltalk, terminating processes which have been started is equally as important. The class **BlockClosure** provides a way of doing this in the form of a method called **valueNowOrOnUnwindDo:** . If you send this message to a block with another block as the parameter, the system will execute the first block, and then the second, *even if the first block results in an exception*. This is very useful for keeping things tidy during development—making sure you don't end up with hundreds of open files, windows, or processes running.

Another way to avoid these problems is to encapsulate the opening of a file, or the spawning of a process, in your own method. Make sure you keep a reference to the file or process (say in an instance variable), and each time you invoke the method, check whether a file is open or a process running, and close it or kill it *before* opening another.

Modifying System Classes

Smalltalk's provision of the entire set of source-code for its implementation explicitly gives you permission to modify the system classes. This is a very powerful facility, and like all such facilities it should be treated with respect. It is absolutely *not* the case however that you should *never* modify a system class.

If you want to add simple functionality, such as new features in the development tools, you should go right ahead. This kind of modification by programmers is what has made the development environment as powerful as it is, so if you think you can improve it further, don't hesitate. If you don't like something, change it.

If you're planning on making modifications to some of the more fundamental classes such as **Object** or **Behavior**, you might want to be more circumspect. There are two dangers—you might break the system, and you might put in changes which are incompatible with someone else's changes.

Look at whether you can achieve the effect you want without modifying the system classes. Look also at how the change you want to make might interact with other changes. Finally, consider how serious you are about changing the way Smalltalk behaves in fundamental ways. If after taking these considerations into account you still want to modify the system classes, then go cautiously ahead.

One of the most powerful features of Smalltalk is the ability to *extend* the language if you wish. You can (and people do) add persistent storage mechanisms, create distributed object systems, change the way the UI works, even change the way inheritance works, all by modifying the system classes. The designers of Smalltalk intended this to be possible. Just remember the kind of responsibility you're exercising.

Other Things to be Careful With

If you browse the class hierarchy, especially in **Object**, **Behavior** and **Class**, you will find all sorts of useful methods. There are one or two of these that you should be careful about using though. Chief amongst them are **perform:** and **become:**. Both of these are very powerful methods—we've already looked at how **perform:** permits and enables the writing of 'pluggable' classes. The **become:** method swaps the state of the object receiving the message with the object sent as a parameter. Both of these methods have their place, but if you find yourself wanting to use them you should stop and ask 'Do I have a good reason for doing this?' If the answer is 'Yes', then go ahead. If the answer is 'No', you should think carefully before using them. The **perform:** method can be slow and makes your code essentially untraceable. The **become:** method never does quite what you expect, and is also costly of resources.

Using Comments

Just like almost all other programming languages, Smalltalk provides a way of putting comments into your code. Also as in other programming languages, carefully chosen comments greatly enhance someone else's ability to understand your code (and your own ability, a few weeks, months, or years later!). However, the reverse is also true. Inappropriate comments can be worse than useless. Smalltalk provides two places you can put comments—inside methods, and attached to classes.

Comments can be embedded into the code of a method using pairs of double-quotes (**""**). It's generally a good idea to put a comment right at the top of each method to describe what the method is for, perhaps what parameters it takes (although that should be obvious if you've named the method and its parameters carefully), what value it returns and anything special about the way it is implemented. If you wanted to be even more formal, you could include things like the creator and the date.

A common and very useful way of using comments at the top of methods is to put in an example of the use of the method. This allows anyone browsing your code to just select the example with the mouse and **do it** to see your code work. You'll come across this frequently in the class library, especially in class-methods in the **instance-creation** and **initialize** protocols.

Comments inside a method should say *why* something is happening, not *how* it is happening. 'Increment index' is not a very useful way to comment **index := index + inc**. 'Move on to next employee' is much more informative. With a little care Smalltalk code can itself be made very readable. Too many trivial comments can disrupt this readability.

Be aware that Smalltalk comments don't nest. This means you can't comment-out whole chunks of code in a method just by wrapping double-quotes around them. If there are embedding comments, they then get treated as Smalltalk code by the compiler, with predictable results!

The other Smalltalk comment mechanism allows you to put a descriptive piece of text into each class. You do this by selecting **comment** from the *operate* menu of the class pane (second from left) in the system browser. You can browse the comment of an existing class, or add one into your own class. Just type what you want and use **accept**. Once you get used to looking at the class comments in the class library to help you understand what the system classes do, you will realise how other users of your classes will thank you for commenting them in a similar way!

Writing Efficient Code

Just as in all programming languages, the efficiency of code written in Smalltalk varies widely. However, it is frequently the case that for historical reasons a great deal more concern is expressed about the efficiency of Smalltalk systems than systems written in other languages. Luckily, there are a few considerations which if taken into account, allow the writing of code in Smalltalk which is every bit as responsive as code in other languages. Not many of these are unique to Smalltalk.

First, consider what you mean by 'efficient'. Do you want your code to execute more quickly, or consume a smaller amount of memory. Are you prepared to sacrifice readability (or reusability) for efficiency? Second, remember that there is no substitute for using the right algorithm. Think carefully about whether you've actually structured your functionality in an efficient way. Third, Smalltalk provides some very useful tools for assessing the efficiency of your code, and tracking down inefficient implementations. We'll look at these techniques in the next chapter.

It is helpful to avoid certain operations which are always inefficient no matter what language you use. For example, you should avoid precomputing values which you may never need. *Lazy evaluation* is the name given to the technique of leaving the computation of some value until it is actually needed. Object-oriented programming allows you to encapsulate this so that the consumer of the value is unaware that it is happening. However, once you've calculated a value, don't throw it away if it might be needed again. OOP also permits this *caching* to be encapsulated. Similarly, avoid recomputing values many times inside a loop. Move the computation outside the loop.

Finally, there are certain operations which are known to be inefficient in Smalltalk. The class **Dictionary** is slower than the class **IdentityDictionary**, because it uses = instead of the much faster ==. Similarly for **Set** and **IdentitySet**. You can use either of these faster classes in place of their slower relatives, provided you're happy that the comparisons for key lookup and set membership will be done using equivalence rather than equality. The dependency mechanism is a slower way of having objects communicate than direct references. So, if speed is important to you, you might be prepared to sacrifice the advantages of dependency to get it. Allocating memory is slow, so don't repeatedly create large objects and throw them away soon afterwards.

All of these inefficiencies can be verified, and potential others explored using the benchmarking, timing and profiling tools provided in the development environment. If you're in doubt about the efficiency of your code, make full use of these tools. They can help you bring about dramatic improvements.

Summary

What we have looked at in this chapter is a set of *guidelines* for some aspects of translating your object designs into working Smalltalk code. Most of these reflect the coding style used by experienced Smalltalkers, and hence the style you will see used throughout the standard class library. In fact the system class library is one of the best places to look for further examples of good Smalltalk style.

We've looked here at the naming conventions which make Smalltalk code more readable, ways of isolating access to instance variables, constants and classes to improve modularity, and ways of structuring methods elegantly. We've also considered some standard ways of coding elements which appear in many designs, looked at some 'gotchas', described how to write useful comments and talked about writing efficient code.

If you adopt these guidelines, you should find that your code integrates better into the class library, and is more usable by you and others. Most Smalltalkers find the techniques we've talked about fit most circumstances. However, if you have a good reason for doing something different, that should be your guide.

In the next chapter we'll consider how you can actually work with the system to find out more about what it's doing and integrate your code into it.

Using the Development Tools

The Smalltalk development environment and the tools it provides are one of the main contributors to the power of Smalltalk. However, once you've learnt about the basic facilities, it's very easy to get stuck there. You may have enough knowledge to keep you going and make you as productive as you were in a conventional language, and yet you're only using a fraction of the facilities which are available!

The purpose of this chapter is to remind you of the basics, but more importantly to encourage you to explore some of the 'advanced' features of the development tools. Because this is a book on Smalltalk, we'll be concentrating on the *programming* tools in *VisualWorks*, rather than the user-interface development tools, or the database tools (although the same principle of trying to make use of more than just the basics still applies). These tools are used not only for writing your own code, but also for exploring the system code. They're also used for debugging, but that's an important enough subject that we'll leave it to the next chapter, which deals exclusively with debugging techniques.

Using Browsers

The browsers provided in the development environment are your window on the class hierarchy. Remember that this includes both the standard class library, and your extensions to it—your program. We introduced the mechanics of using the various browsers in Part I—*The Science of Smalltalk*. By exploring the system, or reading the manual, you will have discovered lots more. We'll look here at how to make the best use of these very flexible tools, and how to really open up your view of the classes in the system.

The first and most obvious thing is to use plenty of browsers. It's surprising how many people struggle on, flitting around the system with just one system browser open. It depends on the size of your screen of course (and you'll already have discovered that with Smalltalk, the bigger the better), but if you're only using one browser at a time, you're really not making the most of the environment.

If you're exploring the system, you might like to try having at least two system browsers open, covering your screen. That way you can use one to concentrate on whatever you're exploring, and the other to pop out and explore the related things you always need to look at when you want to track something down.

Remember too that there are several other kinds of browser. If you find yourself using a system browser to look at the classes in only one category, try using a category browser (use **spawn** from the *operate* menu in the list of categories). This could save you valuable screen space by not displaying the list of categories, although you have to get used to the slightly different layout. Similarly there are class browsers, protocol browsers and method browsers. Each of these jettisons one level of the organisation of the class library, again saving screen space and letting you focus on just what you need to work on. If you're working particularly hard on a single method, and keep coming back to it, why not keep a method browser open on it?

If you want to look at the class hierarchy, you can select **hierarchy** from the *operate* menu of the class list. However, if you want to browse the classes structured according to the inheritance hierarchy (instead of according to the categories), you must select **spawn hierarchy** to open a hierarchy browser. If you especially like looking at hierarchies, you may like the *full browser* which comes as part of the *Advanced Programming ObjectKit*. It cleverly combines a category-based view of the class library, with the ability to see the inheritance hierarchy and browse the methods which are inherited by, as well as implemented by a particular class.

One small warning is important when you use more than one browser. If you alter the code of a method in one browser, and you've also got other browsers open on the same method, those other browsers will not automatically update themselves to reflect the new method definition. If you go to one of these browsers, alter the code again and do an **accept** operation, you'll lose your earlier changes. It pays to be careful about this, so as not to cause yourself undue frustration.

Finding Your Way Around

One of the most important things you need to be able to do confidently in Smalltalk is to navigate your way around the code in the system. The development environment provides all sorts of ways of doing this. In fact, just about every way of looking up something—that any developer has ever found useful—has been included in the development environment. The only apparently useful thing which you can't do is to search your source-code for a particular string of characters, especially as part of a comment. However, because Smalltalk knows a lot more about the context of your source than would be the case in some other languages (it knows whether something is a message, a reference to a variable, a reference to a class and so on), the lack of this facility is not really a problem.

Most of the navigation and search facilities we're going to look at are accessed via the various browsers. All of these are available from the system browser, and an appropriate subset is available from each of the other types of browser. Some of these commands are also available from the launcher, under the **Browse** menu.

The diagram below shows a stylised system browser, and indicates the commands which we're interested in from each menu. There are lots of other commands in each of these menus of course. Hopefully you will have found out what most of these other commands do by now (if not, why not?). The idea here is to encourage you to try some of the navigation commands.

Starting on the left in the category pane, there is the **find class...** command. You can use this to move the browser to look at any class you know the name of. This sounds trivial, but remember that when

The navigation and search commands of the system browser.

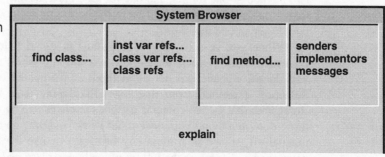

you're prompted for the classname, you can use asterisks (∗) as wildcards. Not only does this save you some typing if you know the name of a class (and lower the risk of making a crucial typo), it also allows you to search for classes by guessing part of their names. Once you get used to the naming conventions of Smalltalk (and especially if you follow the advice in the previous chapter), you'll be able to use this fact to discover classes which do the kinds of things you're looking for.

Next, once you've selected a class, the menu in the class list allows you to search for references to its instance variables, references to its class variables, or indeed references to the class itself. Select one of the first two, and you'll be prompted for the name of the variable you want to search for references to. All three commands then perform a search, and open up a special kind of browser (like the one in the diagram on the next page) showing you all the methods in which a reference to the variable or class was found. This kind of browser is called a *method list browser* and is used to display a set of methods related by the fact that they were produced in response to some search query. You'll see this kind of browser quite frequently. Remember that it has all the same code development facilities in the code pane as every other kind of browser.

You should be aware that there are circumstances in which these 'references to' commands will not catch all references. These circumstances arise when a reference is only visible at run-time and not in the static code. For example, if at run-time you put a class object into another variable (in addition to the well-known global variable it normally lives in), and then start referencing that, you cannot expect the browser to find those references (it's not looking for that name). Of course, you can always search for references to that variable instead. Another case occurs where you follow the advice given in the previous chapter, and only directly access a variable in one accessing method (or two methods—one for get, and one for set). Then the only references to that variable you can find will be in the accessing methods. We'll see how to get around this shortly.

When you've selected a class, you can use the **find method...** command in the protocol pane *operate* menu to produce a (sometimes very large) alphabetical list of methods implemented by that class. Selecting a method from that list will display it in the browser. Remember that the list contains methods *implemented* by the class, not those *inherited* by it. You must either work your way up the hierarchy manually (perhaps in a hierarchy browser) or use the full browser mentioned earlier to see the full set of methods a class *understands*.

The right-most menu contains possibly the most useful commands

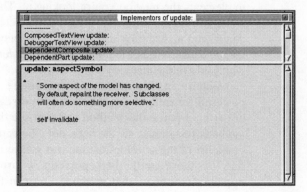

A method list browser,
produced by asking who
implements '`update:`'

for tracking down how things work within the system. If you're looking at a particular method, selecting **senders** will pop up a browser showing you all the places that particular method name (selector) appears in a message expression. This is the way to find references to a variable via accessing methods. *Warning*: the system can't tell whether the expressions it shows you will actually invoke the method you're looking at. This is because that depends on the class of the object the message is sent to—something that isn't known until run-time (remember polymorphism? If not, look back at chapter 2). However, you will get a good idea of which messages could invoke your method, and you'll also be able to see if your method is never invoked.

By using the **senders** command repeatedly, you can work your way 'backwards' through the code, seeing which methods send a particular message, then seeing who invokes *those* methods and so on. This is a very useful way of exploring the system code.

There is another 'gotcha' here though. If you've used **perform:** to invoke a method, that reference to the method is essentially invisible to the development environment. At best, the method's name just appears as a literal symbol in the source-code (at worst, it gets created at run-time). Because it is not syntactically a selector, it can't be seen by the **senders** command.

You might like to consider going through your code occasionally, using the **inst var refs...** and **senders** commands to find and then remove 'dead' variables and methods (assuming you don't have methods which are only invoked via **perform:**). This is another way in which you can contribute to making your code more readable by others.

The **implementors** command will show you every class which implements the method you're looking at. This can be useful if you're trying to find out who else, other than the class you're looking at, you could send a particular message to. Remember though, that you'll see the *implementors*, not the bigger list of *'understanders'* (all the classes which inherit the method).

Finally in this menu, the **messages** command is extremely powerful for following a sequence of message passes. Suppose you're browsing a particular method and you see that it invokes some other methods (as almost all methods do!). Selecting **messages** will show you a list of the selectors the method you're looking at uses. Choosing one of these will then pop up a browser showing all the implementations of that method. You can then pick the one you're interested in, browse the code and use **messages** again to follow the implementation to wherever what you're looking for actually happens. Very often, methods in Smalltalk will simply call a more general version of themselves. This can repeat several times before anything really gets done. The **messages** command makes it very easy to follow these chains of message sends. In effect, whilst **senders** allows you to follow invocations backwards, **messages** allows you to follow them forwards

The last browser menu command we'll cover is in the *operate* menu of the code pane. If you select a piece of the code in a method using the mouse, and then choose the **explain** command, the system will think for a moment and then produce an 'explanation' of whatever you've selected. You have to choose a reasonably logical piece of the method (you can't pick a random sequence of characters), but if you're lucky you'll get a piece of text telling you that what you selected is an instance variable, or a class variable, or a method selector, or anything else.

You should note a couple of things about the explanation. First, the system rather rudely inserts it into the code you're browsing. However, it does make sure that the text it inserts is selected, so you can just hit the <delete> key to get rid of it. Second, the explanation will usually include a snippet of Smalltalk code which, if you evaluate it, will probably pop up another browser with more information about the thing being explained. The **explain** function even makes sure that its explanation is structured into comment and code so you don't have to select a subpart of it. You just follow an **explain** command with a **do it** if you want more information. Then you can still hit <delete> to get rid of the explanation. This has to be one of the cleverest features of the browsers and, like the **messages** command, you should use it regularly.

One last tip to do with browsers (or in fact, any code view). There are a few short cuts which the system helpfully provides. The manual contains a full list, but here are the most useful two. If you want to put parentheses around any expression, just select the expression with the mouse, hit the <escape> key and then type the open parenthesis character. The system automatically brackets the expression with parentheses.

This technique works for other 'bracketing' characters as well (**"**, **'**, **[,{,<**). You can undo this by selecting a bracketed expression (*not* including the bracketing characters), and typing <escape> followed by the opening bracket character. The system will automatically remove the brackets. The second short cut is that if you type <control>–t or <control>–f in a code view, the system will automatically insert **ifTrue:** or **ifFalse:** . Once you get used to these short cuts, you'll wonder why your other editors don't have them!

Using Inspectors

What the browser tools are to classes, inspectors are to instances. By making liberal use of inspectors (as in the diagram below) you can get a very good idea of what the instances your code creates look like, and what they are up to.

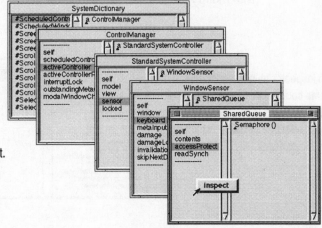

Using a 'chain' of
inspectors to find and
inspect a particular object.

There are several ways of opening an inspector. Selecting an expression with the mouse, and choosing **inspect** from the *operate* menu will evaluate the expression and open an inspector on the result. Remember that an expression can be a single object. For example, just selecting the name of a global variable typed in a workspace and doing **inspect** from the *operate* menu, will open an inspector on the object the variable contains.

Once you've got an inspector open, selecting a variable in the inspected object will allow you to pop up another menu and open a new inspector on that object. This is the key to good usage of inspectors. By repeatedly selecting a variable and opening a new inspector you can follow 'chains' of objects to see how they relate, and find the object you're looking for. Even if you have to open twenty inspectors or more, that's OK. Just close the ones you don't need, carefully keeping the one you wanted open.

You can almost always find the object you're looking for by following chains of object references. The difficult part of this process can be getting the first inspector open. One way around this is to remember that you can get an inspector open by sending the message **inspect** to any object. This is useful during debugging when you'd like to take a look at an object that comes into being inside your code. Just insert an expression like **myObject inspect** into the appropriate method. Using inspectors during debugging is covered in more detail in the next chapter.

Another way around the problem of getting the first inspector open is to modify the *window* menu to allow you to inspect the model, view,

An inspector being used to execute some code, in this case to pick out all the objects in the **Smalltalk SystemDictionary** which are actually classes.

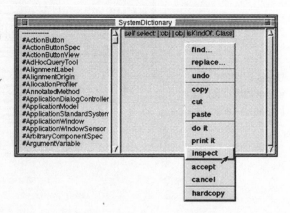

or controller of any window you've got open. This is an interesting exercise in itself. Once it's done, you will find it an amazingly useful way of exploring the system, especially the construction of the system's and your own user-interfaces. It's not a hard thing to do, but to help you you'll find a 'model answer' at the end of this chapter .

Don't forget that you can also execute code in an inspector. The code is executed in the context of the object being inspected. So, if you want to send a message to the object, send it to **self**. Just type the expression in the right-hand pane of the inspector and use **do it**, **print it**, or **inspect** from the *operate* menu, as in the diagram on the previous page.

Using Workspaces

Workspaces are very useful 'scratchpads'. You should use them to try out little fragments of code, or to keep hold of the expressions you need to fire up your applications. Just like all the other tools in the development environment, you can have as many open as you need. You can also change the title of a workspace window by using the **relabel as...** command on the *window* menu.

Sadly, you cannot save the contents of a workspace window, except as part of a saved image. This can be inconvenient, but a way around this is to create one or more 'scratchpad' methods in a class, put the code which was in the workspace into these methods, and then file-out the class. This might be one of your existing classes if the code that was in the workspace is particularly relevant to testing or exercising that class. Alternatively, you could create a special class just to hold this test code.

If you're writing self-contained fragments of code in a workspace, you can define temporary variables in just the same way as you would in a method—by using vertical bar (|) characters. These variables only last for as long as a single **do it**, **print it**, or **inspect** though. If you need to keep the objects you're playing with for a little longer, there's nothing really wrong with using global variables. Just assign the result of an expression to a variable beginning with an upper-case letter, and the system will ask you if you want to define it as a global. Later, if you want to get rid of your globals, inspect the global variable **Smalltalk**. This contains an instance (in fact, the only instance) of a class called **SystemDictionary**. You should be able to find your variables and remove them using the *operate* menu in the left-hand pane. It's helpful to prefix all your globals with the same thing (by calling them **MyView**,

MyFile, **MyWidget** for example) so that they are easily found.

Remember that almost every text view in the system can be used as a workspace. If you need to quickly type and evaluate an expression (such as **MyClass initialize**) just type it anywhere—in a workspace, in a browser, in a debugger, in the transcript. After you've evaluated it, you can just use **cancel** or the <delete> key to get rid of it if necessary. This is much quicker than looking for an open workspace, or opening a new one.

In older versions of *VisualWorks* (prior to 2.0) and in *ObjectWorks*, there was something called the *system workspace*. This contained all sorts of useful code snippets of code for doing the sorts of functions *VisualWorks* 2.0 now provides from the menus in its launcher. If you're using one of these older Smalltalks, it's worth investigating the system workspace.

Tuning the Performance of Your Code

In the previous chapter we looked at some coding techniques which can improve the efficiency of your code. We'll look here at the tools which help you identify areas which need improvement, and allow you to prove you were able to improve them.

The performance of your code depends on two factors—how efficient your code is, and how fast the machine it's running on is. The *VisualWorks* development environment provides three ways to measure these things—timing, benchmarking and profiling. The last two are part of the *Advanced Programming ObjectKit*, so if you don't have this optional extra, you'll only be able to listen to the theory.

Timing code

You can time how long Smalltalk takes to execute any piece of code by evaluating the following expression and printing or inspecting the result. Simply substitute the code you want to time for the comment in the block. Use the expression to compare different ways of doing things.

```
Time millisecondsToRun: ["Your code goes here."].
```

Remember that there are a number of factors which can drastically impact the time it takes to run the code. These include whether the methods you invoke are in the method cache, and whether part or all of your image is swapped out (if you have virtual memory). So like all such scientific tests, it's a good idea to repeat it several times and take the best, worst, or average value as appropriate. You could also write the block to execute your code many times (say 1000) and divide the resulting time appropriately.

Benchmarking

In order for you to be able to assess the underlying performance of the computing platform on which your code is running, *VisualWorks* provides a convenient set of benchmarks which you can run. These test all kinds of features of your system, and then report the results. You can control which benchmarks are run and how the results are reported. You can use the benchmarks to compare how your system performs differently when you alter the platform configuration (change memory or processor speed). You might also want to compare the performance of the platform on which you might be delivering your application against the performance of the platform on which you're developing it.

Profiling

The third kind of performance assessment tool *VisualWorks* provides is the profiler. There are actually two profilers—a time profiler for exploring where time is being spent in your code, and an allocation profiler for exploring where memory is being allocated in your code. Both of these profilers act on a block of code which you provide to them. They run the code many times, and use a statistical sampling technique to monitor what is happening. Because of this, you should make sure you read the accompanying documentation in order that you get the number of repetitions and the sample size right to get valid results.

A hierarchical time profile produced by the time profiler.

```
100.0 ControlManager>>restore
   77.7 ControlManager>>checkForEvents
   22.3 OrderedCollection>>reverseDo:
     22.2 [] in ControlManager>>restore
     22.2 ScheduledWindow>>refresh
       21.8 ScheduledWindow>>extentEvent:
         21.8 BlockClosure>>valueNowOrOnUnwindDo:
           21.8 [] in ScheduledWindow>>extentEvent:
```

The profilers produce results in the form of a hierarchical breakdown similar to the one shown in the diagram on the previous page. You can browse around this using the tool provided in order to understand what's happening. The breakdown shows times or allocations as a percentage of the total. You can open out (plain text) or collapse (bold text) parts of the breakdown in order to help in your exploration.

The diagram shows the results of running the profiler on a piece of system code, but if you use the profiler on your own code you could well have some surprises as to where the system is spending its time. By using the profiler, and acting on the results, great improvements are possible. However, do make sure you profile your code both *before* and *after* you change it. That way you'll know that you really are getting an improvement, and you'll know exactly what the extent of that improvement is.

Managing Your Image (or how not to lose your work!)

The Smalltalk development environment provides very powerful ways to develop applications. By using it to the full, it's possible to be very productive. It's also possible to lose all your work in a moment if you don't take some simple precautions! The advice in this section is based on bitter experience.

There are some very powerful code management tools available for *VisualWorks*, but if these are too complex or expensive for your immediate needs you can do a perfectly good job with the facilities included in *VisualWorks*. So, Smalltalk provides two ways to save work—the 'save-image' facility, and file-out files.

The first rule is to use the 'save-image' facility. Use it often—especially just before you make a crucial change to the system. Provided you have a reasonably fast computer and your image isn't too big (so that it doesn't take too long to save), you should do a 'save-image' *at least* every half hour. Also, do one *after* every change which you don't want to have to repeat, and *before* doing anything that could damage the system. This includes redefining any of the system methods, especially if you're modifying the way the user-interface works. It's very easy to throw yourself into a loop from which you can never recover by damaging the code which deals with the opening of windows, causing the system to try to open a notifier to tell you, causing it to try to invoke the damaged code, causing it to try to open a notifier... . Before you know it, your screen is covered with notifiers which you can't get rid of!

As well as using the 'save-image' facility, you should make use of the file-out facility to keep copies of your finished code outside an image. This makes sure that you can rebuild your image from scratch should this prove necessary. In fact, it's quite a good idea to rebuild your image regularly (perhaps as often as every day), just to make sure that you're not relying on odd instances lying around which you no longer know how to recreate, and to tidy-up any garbage generated during development which the garbage collector fails to reach.

Another important thing when managing your image is *never* to delete your changes file. This file, one of which you'll have noticed goes along with every image file, contains all the source-code you have added or modified. Whenever you change a method, the new source code is added to the end of the changes file. Any old version which may have been in the file remains in the file. In effect, this means that you've got a log of the history of the changes you've made. This log includes **do it**s which have a permanent effect on the image (for example, defining global variables).

Should your image become damaged (and it's not hard to do), you can use a tool called the *change list* (see diagram below) to repair it. This is one of the most arcane tools in the system and is somewhat awkward to use, but since it can almost literally save your life, it's well

The change list tool being used to rebuild an image from a changes file.

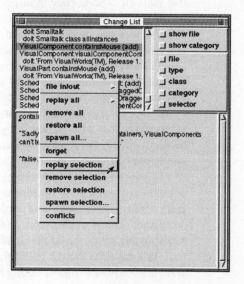

169

worth learning how to use it. Just start up the latest undamaged version of your image, and open a change list from the **Changes** menu in the launcher. Use the **file in/out —> read file/directory** command from the *operate* menu in the top left pane to read into the tool the changes file of the broken image. You can then selectively replay pieces of that file to reconstruct your image. If you're lucky, you'll be able to replay everything you did right up to the moment your image got damaged. Even if you can't, you should get a long way. When you've finished, make sure you do a 'save-image' to a new file straight away (don't overwrite your last working version though).

Summary

Throughout this chapter we've looked at various ways you can enhance your use of the programming tools in the Smalltalk development environment. In particular, we looked at how to make use of the navigation commands in the system browser and its relatives. These enable you to follow message sends both backwards and forwards, which is a big help when you're trying to understand how one of the system classes (or even one of your own) works.

We also looked at getting inspectors open (see below too) and then at using 'chains' of inspectors to explore object instances. Remember that you can execute code in inspectors too.

Workspaces are something that everyone uses differently, but we did consider one or two common ways of using them, and mentioned that any text view in the system can be used as a temporary workspace.

Following on from the discussion of how to write efficient code in the previous chapter, we looked at how to measure the performance both of your own code, and the computer on which you're running it.

Finally, we considered some simple ways of avoiding a catastrophic loss of your work, by using the 'save-image' and file out facilities. If the worst does happen, we looked at using the change list tool to recover your work from the changes file.

If you try some of the things we discussed, you should find that not only are you able to become a more efficient programmer, but that your ability to explore and understand the class library has also increased. These exploration and comprehension skills are vital to realising the full power of the Smalltalk environment.

As it happens though, all of the tools and commands we've looked at here are equally helpful during debugging, and that is the subject of the next chapter.

Appendix: Modifying the Window Menu

We mentioned in this chapter that it is sometimes difficult to get an inspector open on the object you're trying to see. There are several solutions to this problem, and here is one of them.

On the next page there is some Smalltalk code. Type this code into a file (not a browser—just use the Smalltalk file editor, or any other editor) *exactly* as it is listed, and then file it into an image.

Doing this will make the modifications necessary to add a new sub-menu to the *window* menu of all windows. The three commands on this sub-menu allow you to inspect the model of the window, the window object itself, or the window's controller. From there, you should be able to navigate to a particular model object, or a particular view inside the window.

The code works by replacing the **initialize** method of the **StandardSystemController** class with one which puts a new menu, which includes the new sub-menu **inspectMenu**, into **ScheduledBlueButtonMenu** (a class variable). It then adds three new methods to **StandardSystemController** to implement the three **inspect** commands. The last thing the file-in does is to send **initialize** to **StandardSystemController** in order to create the new menu.

Although the code seems to work with versions 1.0 and 2.0 of *VisualWorks* (and versions 4.0 and 4.1 of *ObjectWorks*), like all such things, no guarantee can be given that it will work correctly in your system. Use it at your own risk.

171

```
!StandardSystemController class methodsFor: 'class initialization'!

initialize

  | inspectMenu |

  inspectMenu := PopUpMenu
    labels:'model\window\controller' withCRs
    values: #(#inspectModel #inspectWindow #inspectController).

  ScheduledBlueButtonMenu := PopUpMenu
    labels: 'relabel as...\refresh\move\resize\front
back\collapse\inspect\close' withCRs
    lines: #(1 8 )
    values: ((OrderedCollection withAll:
      #(#newLabel #display #move #resize #front #back #collapse))
          add: inspectMenu; add: #close; yourself).! !



!StandardSystemController methodsFor: 'menu messages'!

inspectModel
      model inspect.!

inspectWindow
      view inspect.!

inspectController
      self inspect.! !



StandardSystemController initialize.
```

Debugging Smalltalk Code

Even if you follow the design approach and the coding guidelines presented in the preceding chapters, you're unlikely to write Smalltalk which is completely free of bugs first time. Luckily, the interactive nature of the Smalltalk development environment makes it very well suited to the task of finding and correcting bugs.

In theory, the main tools—notifiers, inspectors and debuggers—are relatively easy to use. However, there are also a number of 'tips and tricks' which experienced programmers use. These can greatly speed up the process of debugging, and make it altogether less frustrating. This chapter discusses Smalltalk debugging, and then presents a list of common bugs in Smalltalk code with advice on how to detect them and avoid them.

Different Kinds of Bug

We might say that there are three fundamentally different kinds of bug in Smalltalk. The first kind simply involves your code being syntactically incorrect. The compiler (invoked whenever you do an **accept**) will not let syntactically incorrect code be added to the system. Hopefully, your knowledge of the 'science' of Smalltalk is now good enough that you can fix these problems unaided, because we won't be dealing with them here.

The second kind of bug occurs when Smalltalk runs your code, and comes across a problem during execution. In other words, the system finds something it cannot or will not execute. Typically, it will then pop up a *notifier* window. The notifier tells you what the problem is, and gives you the choice of attempting to continue (if possible), opening a debugger window, or aborting execution of your code. This is one of the kinds of bug we shall be looking at.

The third kind of bug is the kind which occurs when your code is correct, but there is something wrong with your *design*. Your program executes fine, but it doesn't do what you wanted it to do. This can happen because you haven't understood how some feature of an existing class works, or it can happen because the design or implementation of one of your classes is wrong. Again, we'll also be looking at how to trace execution of your code and the system's code to track down this kind of bug.

In reality of course, there is also a fourth kind of bug—that which is presupplied in the class library as delivered. Although rare, these bugs do exist, especially in new releases. The techniques presented in this chapter will also help you track down and even (if you're clever) fix these sorts of bug.

General Debugging Principles

When it comes to debugging, Smalltalk has a lot in common with other programming languages. Because the same general principles apply, but also because even experienced programmers forget them sometimes, we'll remind ourselves of these 'rules' first.

The first general principle is to *read* the error message. Although any computer can only tell you the immediate and superficial cause of a problem, and not the underlying origin, it is still worth considering what the error message has to say. It is all too tempting to think 'Oh, an error!' and start searching around your code looking for the problem. Remember, the system is trying to tell you something. At least listen to what it's got to say.

After you've read the error message, slow down. Stop to think about what the problem might be. Debugging is one of those things where it's worth taking the time to *fix it first-time*. If you're not careful, you can find yourself going round and round trying different things out, but not getting any closer to the problem. This is especially true in a system which permits such easy modification and testing of source code as Smalltalk.

The next general principle is not to *assume* anything. Just because you're sure a variable had a particular value at a particular point, or that control flowed through a particular part of your code, doesn't mean that it necessarily did. Check to be sure. Again, the Smalltalk environment makes this bit easy.

One way of forcing yourself to do this kind of checking is to get some help from someone else. The more cynical and difficult to convince this person is the better, but it's well known that even a 'cardboard cut-out' can help force you through the reasoning process that leads you to finding your bug. Just the act of explaining your system to someone else, or drawing diagrams of its behaviour, can be very helpful.

Next, remember that as well as using the debugging tools provided, you can build your own debugging code. If it helps to log things to files, or just to print things to the transcript window, take the time to do it. You can even construct more complex 'monitors' and 'triggers' if you want to. Although this can be painful in some languages, Smalltalk actually makes it quite easy.

Another thing which Smalltalk makes easy is the construction of *stubs*. You can define a method which has the right name and parameters as a method you will eventually write, but not include the final implementation. You can either just return a 'canned' fixed-value, or put in a halt (see shortly) and use the debugger to manually fill-in the value you want the method to return.

Finally, you *should* be trying to build, test and debug small pieces of your system anyway. However, if you hit problems, it's helpful to break your code down into even smaller independent pieces and check them out separately. If that doesn't work, try building a specific test case. Again, it's worth investing the time and effort to do this, just to know once and for all why something doesn't work.

Using Notifiers and Debuggers

Probably the first thing you'll know about a bug in your code is that you get a notifier window popping up. Smalltalk notifiers are popped up in response to *exceptions*, which arise in 'exceptional' circumstances such as the system not knowing how to deal with a particular message expression. The diagram on the next page shows a couple of notifiers.

In line with the general principles we've just looked at, the first thing you should do is to stop and look at the notifier—don't just close it. Smalltalk notifiers give quite a lot of useful information. Obviously, you get the name of the exception ('Message not understood', 'Division by zero', etc.). You also get a *stack back-trace* which shows you exactly what was happening up to the time the exception occurred.

Each line in the back-trace shows a message being sent, starting at the bottom and working up to the top where the error occurred. On every line you'll see the name of the class of the object which *received*

175

Notifiers from *VisualWorks* 2.0
(front) and an earlier version of
Smalltalk (behind). Both were
generated when the system
realised that `nil` doesn't
understand the message
`wibble`.

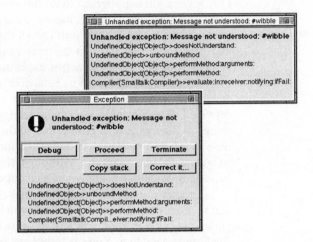

the message, then the name of its superclass which actually implements
the method (in parentheses), and then the method selector itself (after
the **>>**). In other words, each line looks like this:

ReceiverClass(ImplementorClass)>>messageSelector

The very top thing on the stack back-trace will be Smalltalk raising the
exception (yes, you actually get to see the code which generated the
error message!). This means that you're almost always interested in the
second line down. This is where the immediate cause of the error is.
The back-trace will tell you the name of the method in which the error
occurred, or **unboundMethod** if the error happened during a **do it**,
print it, or **inspect**.

Underneath the second line down are all the messages on the stack
leading up to the error. Remember that you are looking at a call-stack.
This means messages which were sent prior to the exception, but which
have already returned, won't be visible to you here (even though they
may be the ultimate cause of the bug).

The other thing to remember is that Smalltalk doesn't make any
distinction between 'its' code and 'your' code. They are one and the
same as far as the system is concerned. This means that the stack back-
trace could easily consist of a mixture of your code and code from the
class library. So, don't be concerned if you don't recognise all the code
that's being shown to you. The diagram on the next page shows a
couple of examples of this phenomenon.

Two possible
combinations of
your code and
the system's
code in a stack
back-trace.

Unhandled Exception
Exception raised
Your code (exception occurs)
Your code
...
System code
System code
...

Unhandled Exception
Exception raised
System code (exception occurs)
System code
...
Your code
Your code
...

As you will see, you may be presented with a stack in which a fair bit of system code leads up to your code starting to run, with the exception happening in your code. This is especially true of exceptions resulting from **do it**s in a workspace.

The other situation is where your code invokes some method in the class library, which then invokes a potentially large number of other methods in the class library, before the exception eventually occurs in a system method. This doesn't mean you've found a system bug! Instead, it means you've done something in your code which led to a problem which wasn't detected until the system eventually tried to do something forbidden in its own code (like access an element which isn't present in a **Collection**).

After you've looked at the error message and the stack, the next thing to do is to decide whether you need to open a debugger. Depending on the version of Smalltalk you have, you'll be given the choice to do this either through a pop-up menu, or through push buttons. If you think you know what the cause of the problem is, that's fine. Just close the notifier and go and fix it. If you want to take a closer look at the code that caused the error, examine variables and have the chance to modify the code, then you should open a debugger.

If you decide to open a debugger, make it *big*. You're trying to get a view on what's gone wrong, so there's no point squinting at your code through a tiny little window. Sometimes the default sizes at which *VisualWorks* opens its windows are ridiculously small. We covered the basic use of debuggers in *The Science of Smalltalk*, and it's also covered in the manual. The important thing is to make sure you make full use of the facilities you're given.

You can browse up and down the stack looking at the path the system took through your code. If there's not enough stack for you, you can ask for more via the *operate* menu in the stack pane. Remember that just like in the notifier you could be looking at a mixture of your code and the system's code. If you see system code at the top of the stack, it's worth scrolling down (back in time) to see where your code begins. The interface between your code and the system's is the last chance your code had not to generate an error. This is often where the bug is. Remember though, that your code could have generated the error much earlier (either in the call-stack or outside), with your code happily passing on a bad object until an exception eventually gets raised much later. If the method which actually has the bug in it has *already returned* you won't be able to see it in the call-stack. In this case you'll have to interrupt your code and follow it through manually to find the bug. We'll look at how to do this very shortly.

You can use the two embedded inspectors at the bottom of the debugger to look at the state of instance variables, as well as temporary variables and parameters to methods. Remember that you can also *execute code* in inspectors. If you want to test out how an object responds to a message, make sure one of the inspectors is inspecting it, type an expression, select it and evaluate it.

If you think you can see the source of the problem, you can use the code pane of the debugger just like a browser. You can edit the code and accept it. Be careful though, because if you've got another browser open on the method, and you subsequently go back to using that, you'll put the error straight back into your code! This occurs because browsers do not automatically update themselves when the code they're browsing is changed elsewhere.

Interrupting Your Code

You can interrupt Smalltalk by pressing *<control>–c* This stops whatever is happening, raises a 'User Interrupt' exception and opens a notifier. From there you can open a debugger as usual. It is even possible to do this when the system is 'idle', interrupting Smalltalk's normal processing loop. You might find it interesting to do this, open a debugger, and explore something of how the system works.

There are occasional circumstances when the system will stop responding to *<control>-c* . This is usually because the image is damaged in some way. In this case, try pressing *<shift>–<control>–c* This should open the *emergency evaluator*—a sort of 'last chance' which uses only a minimal amount of the system. From here you get the chance to enter and evaluate a single Smalltalk expression (terminated by <escape> *not* <return>). What you choose will depend on your situation, but here are some useful choices:

Processor activeProcess terminate. (To try to recover.)
ObjectMemory quit. (To give up and kill Smalltalk.)

If you can't work out what you want to type, remember that (in some environments at least) you can start up another Smalltalk image to browse around and decide. There is only one thing you shouldn't do, and that's try to save your damaged image. When you restart it it will be in exactly the same damaged state, and you'll probably have overwritten your earlier work as well!

Inserting Breakpoints

Sometimes you can't see the actual cause of a problem in a debugger popped up as a result of an unexpected exception. This is because the real cause is in some method which has been invoked and already returned. In this case you may want to set a breakpoint in your code, and then follow the subsequent execution path to catch the error.

In Smalltalk, you don't set breakpoints through the debugger. Instead you insert a piece of code into your program which causes a special kind of exception to happen when and where you want it. You can then open a debugger in response to the resulting notifier.

The way you raise the exception is to send the message **halt**. This message is implemented in **Object**, so every single object in the system understands it, and does the same thing—raise an exception. The normal thing to do to set a breakpoint is to put the expression **self halt** wherever you want execution of the code to stop. You can also use the **halt:** message, which takes a string as a parameter, and includes it in the error message. This can help you to know which of the many halts you've inserted in your code has actually been reached!

When a halt happens, you might decide to proceed, but more likely you'll decide to open a debugger. You can then look at the values of variables, and send messages. You can also then use the **step** and **send** buttons to either send the next message, or send the next message and follow it down into its own implementation. If you get fed up single-stepping, you can choose **proceed** from the *operate* menu.

You can, if you wish, insert a **self halt** into the system's code. Be very careful though, because if you put a halt in a piece of code which is needed to raise an exception, used to open a window, or used to enable you to take the halt out again, you will get an endless stream of notifiers! In this case you're likely to have to use the emergency evaluator we've just described.

Sometimes you don't want to halt until a certain condition is true. In that case, you can obviously just test for the condition and halt if it's true. You might also want to halt after you've been through your code a certain number of times. To save yourself having to keep on using proceed, just set up a global variable, keep incrementing it, and halt when it reaches the right value. Finally, you might also only want to halt the first time through the code (perhaps to avoid the streams of notifiers syndrome described above). In this case, create a global variable called something like **DontHalt**, initialise it to **false**, check whether it's false before you even consider halting, and set it to **true** just before you actually halt.

Another way to control whether a halt actually happens is to write a method called something like **conditionallyHalt** (add it to class **Object**). In that method, check some condition (like the shift key being pressed) and only halt if the condition is true. Then, if you use **conditionallyHalt** instead of **halt**, you can control whether your code halts by whether you hold the shift key down. An expression which determines whether the shift key is down:

```
ScheduledControllers activeController
    sensor shiftDown.
```

Tracing Execution

You can follow the path your code is taking by single stepping through it using the debugger. However, this can be tedious if you just want to know whether a particular method got called or what the value of a variable is. In this case, Smalltalk provides the equivalent of the print statements you might insert into a conventional program for debugging. You can print any string to the transcript window by using an expression like:

```
Transcript show: 'Here is a string'; cr.
```

This would print 'Here is a string' followed by a carriage return. The global variable **Transcript** holds an instance of the class **TextCollector** which is the model (in the MVC sense) for the transcript window. Note that you can only send *strings* to the transcript. You can print other objects by sending them the message **printString** first. For example:

180

```
Transcript show: 'anArray is ', anArray
    printString; cr.
```

If you simply want to know whether something has happened, you can even get the system to beep when it does. Just insert the expression below wherever you need it. It is however worth checking whether it works on your particular platform before using it for real. Here's the expression:

```
Screen default ringBell.
```

Other ways of tracing execution include logging events to a file or building up an **OrderedCollection** of 'trace records', capturing the values of important variables as your code executes. This has the advantage that you can easily inspect the collection to see the sequence of things your program did.

Finding Your Objects

Sometimes you will know that your code has created one or more instances of a class, but you don't know where they've gone to. In this case there are a couple of useful messages which you should know about. They are:

```
MyClass allInstances.
MyObject allOwners.
```

The **allInstances** message can be sent to any class. It will trawl through the entire system and return a collection of all the instances of the class. This can be very useful if you've created a single instance of a class which you've lost (especially if it's a runaway **Process** and you want to **terminate** it), or if you believe there are hundreds of instances of a class which are not getting garbage-collected for some reason.

The **allOwners** method, which can be sent to any object, again trawls the entire system looking for references to the receiver. It will answer a collection of other objects which have references (in instance variables or dependencies) to the receiving object. Again, this can be useful for tracking down why some objects aren't getting garbage-collected.

Note that both of these methods are extremely resource intensive, taking several seconds to complete in an average size image. Because of this you should think very carefully before you design an application which uses them as a matter of course, although they remain very useful during debugging.

Debugging Dependencies

We observed in an earlier chapter that dependency relationships between objects are more difficult to debug than ordinary relationships. This difficulty arises for two reasons—the way dependents are held, and the way they are used.

First, the dependency mechanism as implemented in **Object** (but not as re-implemented in **Model**), doesn't use an instance variable to hold dependent objects. Instead, it uses a class variable holding a dictionary full of all the objects which have dependencies. This means that the dependents of a subclass of **Object** are less easy to see in an inspector than those of a subclass of **Model**. The way around this 'invisibility' of dependents is to remember that you can execute code in inspectors. If you are looking at an object with an inspector and you want to see its dependents but there is no dependents instance variable, just type the expression **self dependents** in the right-hand side of the inspector and **inspect** it. That will give you an inspector on a collection of the object's dependents.

The second problem is that dependency causes messages (updates) to get sent to other objects whenever a change message is sent to an object which has dependents (if you're not sure about this, look back at chapter 8). These update messages can cause arbitrarily large amounts of other code (*your* code) to run, depending on what the 'update' methods do. However, when you are single-stepping in the debugger, you will miss these update messages and so miss your code being run, if you just use **step** to execute a change message. The entire dependency mechanism will fire, resulting in the execution of 'update' methods, which in turn will invoke other code, none of which you will see. To see these messages getting passed, you must use **send** when you execute a change message whilst single-stepping in the debugger. You must keep using **send** to work your way up through the system code which runs until you eventually see your update method getting run.

Common Bugs in Smalltalk Programs

Lots of different kinds of bug find their way into Smalltalk programs. However, there are a number of them which tend to appear again and again. Some of the bugs are easy to spot—some of them are more insidious. The last section of this chapter contains descriptions of some of the traps most Smalltalk programmers have fallen into (sometimes more than once) at one time or another. Even if reading about these bugs doesn't help you avoid them, it may help you recognise and fix them more quickly on the day *you* get caught by them! You might like to refer back to this section if you ever find yourself puzzling over a particularly difficult bug.

The `doesNotUnderstand:` message

This has to be the most common error message you will ever see when a notifier pops up. It has one of two causes: you sent the right message to the wrong object; or you sent the wrong message to the right object. You can tell which situation you're in by reading the message in the notifier carefully. Note that the message name will be preceded by a `#` because the system treats it as a symbol. Can you tell where you are in your (or the system's) code? If you can, which do you recognise as correct—the message which was sent, or the object which received it?

The most common situation in which the right message goes to the wrong object is when you try to send a message to `nil`. In this case you'll be told that `UndefinedObject` (the class of which `nil` is the only instance) does not understand the message. This typically occurs because something hasn't been defined, initialised, or assigned to. It can also occur when a previous message (either in a cascade, or a previous expression) returned `nil`, instead of the right thing. You'll have to use the stack back-trace to track this down.

The wrong message going to the right object can be more complicated. In theory, the compiler won't let you accept any messages which aren't implemented by any class. This means that the message being sent must be understood by instances of *some* class. What's probably happened is that you've made a typo, converting the message you meant to type to another legal message. A common way for this to occur is if the bracketing of an expression is wrong. This can easily happen in complex message expressions, and can be difficult to spot. So, if you get a `doesNotUnderstand:` error which you don't understand, check the way you've got your parentheses arranged.

Problems with copies

In Smalltalk, objects are 'passed by reference'. This means the system does not make copies of objects which are passed as parameters or assigned to variables. It passes or assigns the actual objects. Most of the time, this is fine, but just occasionally, even experienced programmers structure their code in such a way that they make an assumption that a copy is being generated when it isn't.

If your objects seem to be mysteriously altering all by themselves, it pays to consider whether what you think are two *separate* instances of a class, might actually be the same instance. You can check this by getting hold of the two objects (if necessary by grubbing around with the debugger, using inspectors and assigning them to global variables), and sending one of them an == message with the second object as a parameter. For example, to check if **MyRecord** and **MyOtherRecord** are the same instance use:

```
MyRecord == MyOtherRecord.
```

If this expression evaluates to **true**, then these two objects are really only one object. If it evaluates to false, then you've got two distinct objects even if they are '='. (If you're not sure about the difference between == and =, look back at Chapter 6—*The Smalltalk Class Library.*) This same test can be used when you want to check whether multiple references to the same object really are references to the *same* object. Manipulating a copy of an object when you thought you were working with the actual object is also a common source of bugs.

Another problem can occur when you use **select:**, **reject:** or similar messages to build a new collection from an existing one. Although the collection object is new, its contents will be (a subset of) the same objects which are in the existing collection. This can give you a surprise, and cause much frustration, when you modify the objects in one collection, only to find that the objects in the other collection 'magically' change too. They're the same objects!

Using equality (=) instead of equivalence (==)

If you want to test to see if one object *is the same object* as another object, you must use the equivalence test, '=='. Using equality, '=', will give false positive results. Conversely, using '==' when all you wanted was '=' will give false negatives.

Modifying a collection during iteration

Sometimes, it's very tempting to modify the contents of a collection whilst iterating over it. For example, you might want to remove all the elements of a collection whose size is greater than ninety-nine. In that case you could easily write an expression such as:

```
MyCollection do: [:i | (i size > 99) ifTrue:
    [MyCollection remove: i]].
```

This simply won't work. Because you're shrinking the size of the collection whilst iterating over it, the iterator will keep missing out elements. This can be very frustrating until you spot what's happening.

The correct thing to do in this case is to use the **select:** enumeration method to build up a new collection containing just the elements you want, and then replace the old collection with the new one. If **select:** or one of its cousins is really not suitable, then you should create a new collection yourself, and fill it whilst iterating over the old one.

If your system has many references to the old collection which you can't trace and change to a reference to the new collection, consider using a **ValueHolder** (see chapter 10) to hold the collection. Lots of objects can then keep references to the **ValueHolder** (which is long-lived), even though its value (the collection object) keeps being replaced.

Note that it is perfectly safe to alter the 'internals' of an object in a collection whilst you are iterating over it. For example the following code is quite safe and normal. It checks the size of every object in the collection **MyCollection** and sets the size of those which are bigger than ninety-nine, to ninety-nine:

```
MyCollection do: [:i | (i size > 99) ifTrue:
    [i size: 99].
```

Omitting the return operator (^)

It's very easy to miss out the return operator (^) in a method which is supposed to return something other than **self**. If you seem to be sending the right message to the wrong object, check that you're returning the correct thing earlier on in the call-stack.

This error is especially nasty in instance-creation methods, where failing to return the newly created instance will result in the class (which is **self** in a class method) being returned. This will almost certainly cause a **doesNotUnderstand:** exception when you try to send the first message to your 'new' object. Unfortunately these exceptions make it look just like your new object doesn't understand a message it's supposed to, except for the subtle inclusion of the word 'class'. In other words you get the first exception below, but you think that you *see* the second:

```
MyClass class (Object) >> doesNotUnderstand:
MyClass (Object) >> doesNotUnderstand:
```

If your newly created objects don't understand some messages and you can't workout why, check for this one—you could be using a class instead of an instance!

Using '^' in a block

Much as you might like to do so, you can't use a return operator (^) to exit from a block back into the method which is running it. For example:

```
MyBlock := [:colour | (colour > 3)
    ifTrue: [^#red]
    ifFalse: [^#yellow]].
```

If you want to exit a block into the method which is running it, you have to structure your block so that you drop out of the end of it. Remember, the 'return' value of a block is the value of the last expression it contains. So, if you want to control that value, assign it to a temporary variable, and finish the block with the name of the variable in an expression by itself. For example:

```
MyNewBlock := [:colour |  |returnVal| (colour > 3)
    ifTrue: [returnVal := #red]
    ifFalse: [returnVal := #yellow].
    returnVal].
```

If you use a ^ in a block, you will not only return from the block, but also from the entire method. This is fine if that's what you intended. However, if you intended to exit from just the block, then you won't get the intended effect. What's worse, the return does not happen from the method which is *running* the block, but from the method which *created* it. If that method has already returned, then you will get a 'Context cannot return' exception. In other words, **MyBlock** is legal if executed in the method which defined it (in which case the ^'s will cause a return from that method), but not legal if executed in another method not called from that method (in which case you'll get an exception).

Failing to re-execute a block definition

This is more of a problem during development than final code execution, but it can be really infuriating even so. It's especially easy to fall into this trap if you're using classes like **PluggableAdaptor**. The bug applies to the use of blocks, and to a lesser extent other objects which are created in one place and used elsewhere (like menus).

If your code is making a block, keeping it in a variable, and then executing it elsewhere, you must remember that if you change the code which makes the block (changing the block definition), you must *re-execute* that code for the change to occur to the block.

You can get very used to being able to alter *methods*, but not having to create new instances for the changes to be visible. This is not the case with blocks. Just because you alter a block's definition, does not mean the system goes and finds all the blocks which were created with that definition and changes them to the new definition! You can find yourself repeatedly altering a method which defines a block, executing the block in a pre-existing instance and wondering why your changes aren't having any effect. It's because the existing block isn't being changed!

Sending an incorrect control message to a boolean value

It is very easy to try to use some of the control structures which **BlockClosure** provides by mistakenly sending them to a **Boolean** value instead. This has to do with expecting the control structures to be part of the language rather than part of the class hierarchy. In the following example the first expression will generate an error. The second expression is the correct implementation.

```
(MyCount > 10) whileFalse: [MyCount := MyCount +1].
[MyCount > 10] whileFalse: [MyCount := MyCount +1].
```

Summary

You should be able to see by now that debugging Smalltalk code is not all that different from debugging code in any other language. You do have a very complete view of what's happening in your Smalltalk code, but you also need to remember that your code, the system's code and even the debugger, are all living in the same world. Nowhere is the lack of a division between you and the Smalltalk system more apparent than when you're debugging.

The facilities you're provided with are perhaps basic but can be combined in very powerful ways. With a bit of patience and creative thought, you can create your own debugging code, which will tell you virtually anything you need to know about the way your code is behaving. In spite of this, the old guidelines on how to do debugging in any language still apply to Smalltalk. These include reading the error message, slowing down, not assuming anything, writing your own debugging code and developing and debugging only small pieces of your system at one time.

We've looked at a range of techniques that many experienced Smalltalkers use. As you yourself become more experienced in debugging Smalltalk code you'll develop your own techniques, and also start to recognise the signs of certain common bugs early on. We've described some of these in this chapter. Combining your own experience with that related here should rapidly help you to write Smalltalk code with fewer and fewer bugs.

Managing Smalltalk Projects

In the first chapter of this book we looked at how to get started in Smalltalk. We talked about how Smalltalk is different from other languages, and the culture shock which that can cause. We also saw a typical Smalltalk 'discomfort curve' and mentioned various ways to reduce its height and length.

In this final chapter we'll look again at some of the management issues which a move to Smalltalk can raise. Like so many other things, this subject is complex enough to require a whole book all to itself, so we'll be able deal with it only briefly.

We'll look at the software lifecycle, mention something about training and consider how you might organise a team. Then we'll look at the technical issues of configuration management, and metrics and measurement. Finally, we'll end with a reminder of the basic message of *The Art and Science of Smalltalk*.

The Software Lifecycle

Depending on your situation you may be more or less aware of the *software lifecycle*. However, one of the things that developers and managers alike need to appreciate about Smalltalk is that its lifecycle is different. As we said earlier, Smalltalk promotes and safely supports a much more interactive and exploratory programming style than many other languages. You will need to adapt to this new lifecycle if you're to get the benefits which Smalltalk offers. The benefits of more rapid development with fewer resources are probably the ones you wanted when you decided to switch to Smalltalk in the first place. If you fail to adapt your own way of working to suit the new environment, you will probably also fail to get all (or any) of the benefits it can offer.

The main thing to do is to make use of your ability to create rapid prototypes and to iteratively refine them. Remember that in other languages you had to be conservative because of the time it took to code something, or modify it if it was incorrect. This is not nearly such a problem in Smalltalk.

Unless you're in a situation which explicitly demands it (in which case you might want to think carefully about using Smalltalk in the first place), don't over-analyse or over-design your system before you start constructing. Remember the 'grain' of the class library you're trying to make maximum reuse of. Explore it early on. *Try out* your ideas and use what you discover to improve your design. Don't above all try to adopt a 'waterfall' methodology.

However, don't go completely mad. Smalltalk is not an excuse for a free-for-all. The interactive lifecycle can give rise to increases in code bulk as modifications to the system are added. Try to allocate time in your process to regularly go back and polish the code you've already written, removing redundant methods and variables, and generalising it wherever you can.

Training

Having made the decision to start developing in Smalltalk, training is perhaps one of the first things you will consider. Whilst the quality and value for money of any training you may be offered is a matter only you can judge, there are some general guidelines which might help you make a good decision about the kind of training you undertake.

First, make sure you get specific *Smalltalk* training. There are also general object-oriented design and programming courses available. These are probably fine, but no real substitute for Smalltalk-specific training. Don't fall into the common trap of sending developers on a C++ course, or thinking that because they've been on such a course before they will understand Smalltalk. They won't. Also, be aware that it's not necessarily a trivial move from other interactive development systems (such as *Visual Basic*) to Smalltalk. The increase in complexity can be quite a shock!

Second, it can sometimes be worth giving intensive training to a few members of the development team, and then letting them train the others. People learn Smalltalk best by doing it, but having someone else easily available with even a small amount more experience than yourself can be immensely valuable.

Finally, remember that the transition to objects and *Smalltalk* can entail a great deal of fear about loss of skills. People who have become recognised as experts in COBOL or *MS–Windows* programming will suddenly find themselves reduced to the level of beginners. Or rather, they will *feel* as if they have been reduced to the level of beginners. However, with an open mind, and given the time to explore the new paradigm, the same level of skill will rapidly be regained.

Organising the Team

The different lifecycle which Smalltalk encourages, and the different architecture which its programs and systems tend to have, also have an impact on how the development team should be organised. You should be aware of these differences.

To take advantage of the iterative lifecycle of Smalltalk you are likely to need to combine the jobs of analyst, designer and programmer. As we have observed, it is difficult to do design for Smalltalk in the abstract. You need to know what kinds of class exist to be reused before you can start specifying objects and methods. It is also difficult to communicate the design of a Smalltalk class in anything other than Smalltalk, so why bother? What this boils down to is that *everyone* in the team needs to be aware of the application being developed, and be able to play the roles of analyst, designer and programmer as necessary. Equally, *everyone* in the team needs to be more or less familiar with Smalltalk. It really is no good having analysts or designers who don't know *anything* about the target language.

Just as in conventional programming, there are both generators and consumers of code. In Smalltalk the unit of transfer between programmers tends to be the *class*. Individuals will own classes which they design and build, and which they make available to other people for reuse by encapsulation or inheritance. The interfaces between classes must be as clearly defined as before. In Smalltalk though, we tend not to talk about APIs (application program interfaces) between modules, but rather about the *protocol* which different classes support.

It is usually the case that some classes are more reusable than others. These classes, if they are not specific to an application, tend to form a *framework* around which the rest of the application is built. You might like to structure the development team to reflect this by thinking about *framework* developers and *application* developers. If you do things really well, you should come up with a framework which is reusable across many applications.

Reuse is another factor which influences team management. Everyone has a great tendency to trust (or at least understand) their own code more than anyone else's. This tendency naturally works against reuse between individuals. There are at least two ways to mitigate this.

First, increase the knowledge about what is available for reuse. You could try to set up a 'library' of reusable code. It has been suggested that a specific team member should adopt the role of librarian, managing and encouraging the use of these classes. Second, consider explicitly rewarding reuse. How you *measure* reuse is another matter (see later), but if you're still rating a programmer on the number of lines of code he or she *writes* then you are doing little to encourage extensive reuse. Remember it is important to encourage the actual reuse of code rather than just the writing of potentially reusable code.

Configuration Management

One of the areas in which Smalltalk is weakest compared to other languages and development environments is in its support for configuration management. It is an excellent system for a lone programmer developing one version of an application. However, when it comes to multiple programmers trying to work together to develop several versions of an application, Smalltalk as delivered is somewhat lacking.

There are commercial packages which enhance the *VisualWorks* environment to overcome these difficulties. One in particular (*ENVY/Manager* from Object Technology International) is very popular and regarded by many as essential in large (say more than five programmers) projects. However, there are a number of steps you can take to help yourself without investing in a code management package.

First, distinguish between Smalltalk's 'save-image' and 'file-out' mechanisms as ways of saving and sharing code. An image should be something which is private to a programmer. Your image will contain all your bits and pieces, classes and instances, global variables and everything else you need on your workbench during the development process. It's a very powerful facility, and as we've mentioned before you should save your image often, using it as the normal way of making a snap-shot of your work every half an hour or so.

However, you shouldn't *share* your image with anyone else. If you want to transfer code to another developer, use the file-out mechanism to write code into a file, and then have the other person file that code into their own image. This way of sharing code also influences the nature of the units of code which individual programmers can own. You can file-out whole categories, whole classes, whole protocols, or individual methods. Therefore these things are all appropriate units of ownership for different members of a team. It is much more difficult for a team member to own five methods in three different protocols in someone else's class.

The two saving mechanisms (save-image and file-out) can be combined with appropriate splitting of code ownership to produce a basic configuration management process. This process can be administered manually with a little bit of care and responsibility. Here it is:

Start with a *base* Smalltalk image. This need not be the image as delivered out of the box. It can incorporate whatever modifications you feel are absolutely fundamental to your environment—at least set the time zone correctly!

Divide the work so that each programmer preferably owns whole categories of classes. Sometimes individual classes in a shared category will need to be owned, and sometimes even individual protocols and methods. All these are acceptable, but the clearer the divisions you can make, the better the process will work.

Using a shared filesystem (*LanManager*, *Novell*, NFS, etc.), decide on a directory structure where you will keep file-outs of these categories, classes, protocols and methods. Set up permissions so that owners may read and write to these directories, whilst others may only read.

Now, whenever a programmer creates or modifies a unit of code and wants to release it, he or she should file-out that unit to the shared filespace. Every day (or more or less frequently as appropriate) each programmer should start with the base image, and file-in all the additions from the shared filespace. This builds the latest version of the system on which the programmer can work during the day. Each programmer should save their own image privately whenever they feel they've made some progress, but only file out code to the shared area when they're ready to release it.

This simple scheme allows everyone's development to stay in step, and also prevents images becoming very long-lived. Developing using one image for weeks or months is a very bad idea. Images tend to get 'tired' and fragile as they accumulate lots of global variables and other junk as side-effects of the development process. Sharing these defects amongst programmers is especially bad.

There are several ways in which this fully manual scheme can be enhanced. Using the changes log it is possible to tell what parts of the system have been modified. Therefore, it is possible to build code which knows which bits to file-out on demand.

It's also a very good idea to build a kind of boot-strap loader class. This class (the equivalent of a C makefile) can know about all the other files which must be filed-in to build the image. You can write it so that simply filing it in and sending it a message such as **load** will have it file-in all of the rest of the system.

Finally, since the file-outs are simple ASCII files, remember that you could manage them with any other configuration management software (such as RCS) in order to be able to maintain more than one version of your system.

Metrics and Measurement

It is often observed that you can't manage what you can't measure. Unfortunately it is by no means clear *what* you should measure when programming in Smalltalk. To a large extent it depends on what you want to manage or optimise, and it's probably only with experience that you'll be able to decide what is important to you, how to measure it and how to respond to what you measure. What this means is that if you want to control your programming carefully, you need to build up your own history of measurements, recording how they change over time and in response to different conditions.

Here is a list of some of the things that it is possible to measure. None of these measurements is directly supported by *VisualWorks* , but many of them can be programmed with a little ingenuity.

- Lines of code
- Number of methods
- Number of classes
- Lines of code per method
- Lines of code per class
- Methods per class
- Lines of code reused
- Methods reused
- Classes reused
- Instance variables per class
- Instances per class
- Inheritance depth
- Cohesion between methods
- Coupling between classes

Some of these metrics are clearly of more value than others. 'Lines of code' is probably pretty irrelevant, especially as a comparison with other programming languages. You just can't compare your efficiency in Smalltalk against your efficiency in another language by comparing how many lines of code per hour you can write. 'Number of methods' and 'number of classes' are much better measures of how big your system is, and how quickly you're writing it.

'Lines of code per method' is probably a good measure as it will show up methods which are too long (more than about ten lines). 'Methods per class' is less interesting, but 'cohesion between methods' (whether they act on the same set of instance variables) will show up classes which are perhaps fulfilling two or more disjoint needs.

'Methods and classes reused' (either by inheritance or by encapsulation—remember to measure both) is a good thing to be measuring if you want to encourage reuse. Watch out for classes which inherit from another class but don't use many of the features of that class. This may indicate inappropriate inheritance.

'Inheritance depth' is a subtle one as it can be both too shallow (indicating a possible failure to recognise the commonalities between classes), or too deep (inappropriate inheritance leading to unnecessary complexity). 'Coupling between classes' is a measure of how much instances of particular groups of classes tend to interact. This can indicate too great a dependence on the implementation of one class by another class.

Summary and Final Conclusions

This chapter has looked very briefly at some of the people, project and change management issues which a move from a conventional language to Smalltalk development entails. The most important message is that here, as in many other places, Smalltalk is different.

You cannot expect to simply continue your existing process *and* realise the benefits of OOP, interactive development and Smalltalk. You must be prepared for at least some retraining, changes in the combinations of skills developers need and for a period of perhaps intense discomfort. However, having made it this far through the book, you should be well prepared to initiate these changes, and well able to recognise the benefits as you start to see them.

This chapter also brings us to the end of our look at the art and science of Smalltalk and so it's time to reflect on the important things we've considered.

The most important lesson is that a little knowledge can go a long way. The key thing Smalltalk developers need to know is how to *explore* the system. Good Smalltalkers may not necessarily know something, but they'll know how to find it out. We've looked in detail at how to use some of the tools in the *VisualWorks* environment to facilitate and support the exploration process.

This exploration skill needs to be combined with a basic knowledge of the common classes in the system class library, and the way in which they're structured and used. We've looked at some of the common classes and discussed the coding styles and naming conventions which govern their design. We've also considered how to extend the system (because that's what programming in Smalltalk is) in a way which matches this style.

Finally, we've also looked at how the differences between Smalltalk and other more conventional languages change the software development process. In particular we have observed that Smalltalk development is a much more iterative and interactive process than you may be used to. Above all, being sensitive to all these differences should enable you to maximise the return on your investment in Smalltalk. Good luck.

Glossary

This section attempts to provide definitions for many of the words used repeatedly throughout this book. A lot of these words come from object-oriented programming, which like many fields suffers from a certain amount of fuzziness or debate as to what exactly some terms mean. In these cases the definition given is the one normally accepted in Smalltalk, or failing that the one used in this book. Words in *italics* have their own (or related) definitions in the glossary.

Abstract Class A *class* which the designer intended never to have *instances*. In Smalltalk this is by convention—there is no explicit mechanism for enforcing it (although the *class method* **new** may be overridden with **self shouldNotImplement** if desired). Also sometimes called an abstract *superclass*. Compare with *concrete class*.

Accessing Method A *method* intended by the designer to permit access to the otherwise private *instance variables* of an *object*. Accessing (or sometimes just 'access') methods are usually divided into *get methods* and *set methods*.

Adaptor In Smalltalk, an *object* which converts the *messages* sent by one object into those *understood* by another.

Aggregation One of several kinds of relationship between *objects*, in which one object is regarded as being composed of several others.

Aspect In Smalltalk, a particular part, facet or feature of an *object*.

Block   In Smalltalk, a self contained piece of code which is itself an *object*, and which can be created, passed around, and executed any number of times. Blocks may take zero or more *parameters* and have the general form `[:p1 :p2 || temps | "Smalltalk code"]`.

Browser   One of a set of tools in the Smalltalk development environment used for examining, writing and changing Smalltalk *classes*, whether they belong to the *class library* or to the user.

Cascading   In a *message expression*, the sending of multiple messages to the same *receiver*, separated by semicolons (;).

Category   A group of *classes* in Smalltalk which perform related functions, or are otherwise collected together for human convenience when presented in a *browser*. Compare with *Protocol*.

Chaining   In a *message expression*, the sending of a *message* to the *object* which was the *return value* of the previous message.

'Changed' Message   One of several *messages* which can be sent to an *object* (usually by itself) informing it that it has changed, and that it should tell its *dependents* via *'update' messages*.

Class   A special kind of *object* which in Smalltalk acts both as a template for other objects (*instances*) and as a factory for creating them. All objects are instances of a particular class.

Class Library   The set of several hundred *classes* which both come as a part of Smalltalk, and which themselves implement the language and the development environment. Also called the *system library*.

Class Hierarchy   The *tree*-like structure into which all *classes* fit by virtue of their *inheritance* relationship with other classes. Sometimes used as a synonym for *class library*.

Class Method   A *method* designed to be invoked by sending a *message* directly to the *class* which defines it, rather than to an *instance* of that class. Instances do not *understand* class messages. Class methods are only visible when the **class** button of a browser is pressed.

Class Variable   A *variable* defined in a *class* to which the class, its *subclasses* and all *instances* of the class and its subclasses have access.

Collection The general name for a large number of *classes* within the *class library* which implement the notion of a collection of other *objects*. Also the name of the *abstract class* at the top of the *hierarchy* of collection classes.

Concrete Class A *class* which, in contrast to an *abstract class*, is intended by the designer to have *instances*. Most ordinary classes are regarded as concrete classes.

Controller One of the three types of *class* which are part of the *MVC* architecture. Controllers receive input from the user in the form of key-presses and mouse-clicks, and interpret that input in terms of actions performed on *models*.

Dependency An important kind of relationship between *objects* whereby one object can receive information about changes to another object. Dependency relationships are possible between any objects in the system, although they are especially important between members of the *MVC* architecture.

Dependency Mechanism The set of methods in the *class* `Object` and elsewhere, which implement the *dependency* relationship.

Dictionary A kind of *collection* in which one set of objects (the keys) are used to index or refer to another set of objects (the values).

Encapsulation The notion that the internal structure of an *object* is private. In Smalltalk the fact that an object's *instance variables* are only visible to itself (unless *accessing methods* are provided), and the fact that a *method*'s *interface* is separate from its *implementation* are both examples of encapsulation.

File-In A file containing Smalltalk source-code, created via a file-out operation, and which may be loaded into another *image* via a file-in operation.

Get Method A *method* provided by the writer of a *class* to enable users of *instances* of the class to get the value of a particular *instance variable* by sending a message to the instance. Usually has the same name as the instance variable.

Hierarchy An arrangement of *objects* in a *tree*-like structure. In Smalltalk, frequently used as a synonym for *class hierarchy*, although other hierarchies exist (eg. amongst *widgets* in a window).

Implement In Smalltalk, a *class* is said to implement a *method* if the method is actually defined (or redefined) in that class (rather than being inherited). Compare with *understand*.

Implementation The actual definition of a *method* inside a class. Compare with *interface*.

Inheritance A relationship between *classes* by which they are organised into a *hierarchy*. Classes lower in the hierarchy are said to inherit from classes higher in the hierarchy. When a class inherits from another class it receives all that class's *methods* and *variables* and is then able to incrementally define its own additional methods and variables.

Inspector A tool within the development environment which allows a Smalltalk programmer to examine and modify an *instance* object. Compare with *browser*.

Instance A particular occurrence of an *object* defined by a *class*. In Smalltalk, all objects are instances of some class.

Instance Method A *method* which although defined in a *class*, is only *understood* by *instances* of that class.

Instance Variable A *variable* which although defined in a *class*, only appears in *instances* of that class. Every instance of the class has its own separate occurrence of the instance variables defined in the class.

Instantiation The name of the process by which a *class* creates an *instance* of itself.

Interface The name of and *parameters* to a *method*, together with its return value. Compare with *implementation*.

Leaf The *object* at the bottom of a *hierarchy*.

Message The mechanism by which one *object* invokes a *method* in another. A message includes the name of the method to be run and any necessary *parameters*.

Message Expression A combination of *messages* sent to various *receivers*, the result of one message being used as the receiver of, or as a *parameter* to, the next message. In Smalltalk, message expressions always end with a full stop (period).

Method The basic unit of code inside an *object*. Each method has a name, takes zero or more *parameters*, and returns one object. Methods are invoked by sending a *message*, and *implemented* using one more *message expressions*.

Model One of the three types of class which are part of the *MVC* architecture. Models act as repositories for application data and implement application functionality.

MVC Model–View–Controller. A basic architectural building block of Smalltalk in which the functionality of an application with a graphical user–interface is divided among three kinds of object—*models*, *views* and *controllers*.

Notifier A window popped-up by Smalltalk in response to an error or some other exceptional situation.

Object A software entity consisting of a tightly-bound combination of code (*methods*) and data (*variables*). In Smalltalk (where "everything" is an object), the term applies equally to *instances* and *classes*. Also in Smalltalk, `object` is the name of the class at the *root* of the entire *class hierarchy*.

Object-Oriented Built using *objects*, or incorporating some or all of the following principles: *encapsulation*, *polymorphism*, *inheritance*, *instantiation*.

Over-Loading A term used to describe multiple *methods* which although they have the same name, have a different behaviour. In this case the method name is said to be over-loaded. Thus the same *message* sent to different *objects* may have a different effect depending on which method is actually invoked. In Smalltalk this will depend on the *class* of the object *receiving* the message.

Over-Riding The redefinition or replacement in one *class* of a *method* which was *inherited* from its *superclass*.

Parameter An *object* sent as a part of a *message* to provide the *method* being invoked with the additional information needed to run. In Smalltalk, parameters are embedded within method names (*selectors*).

Protocol The set of *methods* a *class understands*. A set of methods which implement similar functions, or cooperate to implement a single function. A set of methods presented together for human convenience in a *browser*. Compare with *category*.

Polymorphism The notion that different *classes* may provide different *implementations* of the same *method*. Thus, the same *message* sent to instances of different classes may have the same effect, but be implemented in completely different ways.

Receiver The name given to any *object* which is being sent a *message*. Compare with *sender*.

Return Value The *object* passed back from *receiver* to *sender* following a completed *method* invocation.

Root The *object* at the top of a *hierarchy*.

Selector The name of a *method*.

Self 'Me'. In Smalltalk, the name given by any *object* to itself. A special kind of pseudo-variable used in expressions when an object needs to send a *message* to itself, which is the only way it has of invoking one of its own *methods* from inside another method.

Sender The *object* originating a *message* being sent to another object.

Set Method An *accessing method* provided by the writer of a *class* to enable users of *instances* of the class to set the value of one of its *instance variables*. This is done by sending the appropriate message with the value as a *parameter*.

Smalltalk-80 An *object–oriented* programming system, developed at *Xerox PARC,* and consisting of a language, a development environment, and an extensive library of *system classes*.

Subclass Any *class* which, when taking part in an *inheritance* relationship with another class, is the class which inherits functionality. In Smalltalk, all classes except **Object** are subclasses of some other class. A class can be both a subclass and a *superclass* if it is in the middle of an *inheritance hierarchy*.

Super Similar to *self*, in that super means 'me'. However, unlike self, when a *message* is sent to super by an *object* the search for the *method* to be invoked begins not in the object's *class*, but in the object's *superclass*. This allows classes to *over-ride* methods *inherited* from their superclass, but also invoke the over-ridden method in the over-riding method's *implementation*. Using self instead of super in this case would cause an infinite loop because the over-riding and the over-ridden methods have the same name.

Superclass Any *class* which when taking part in an *inheritance* relationship with another class, is the class which the other class inherits from. All classes except those at the 'leaves' of the inheritance tree are superclasses even though they are probably also subclasses. Note that superclasses are not necessarily *abstract classes*.

System Class Any *class* which is a part of the standard *system library* of classes.

System Library A synonym for *class library*.

Tree In Smalltalk, another name for *hierarchy*.

Understand An *object* is said to understand a *message* if it either *implements* or *inherits* a method which can be invoked in response to the message. Because of inheritance an object may understand a large number of messages which it does not itself implement.

'Update' Message One of a number of *messages* received by an *object* when another object on which it is *dependent* is sent a *'changed'* *message*.

Variable A storage location for an object. In Smalltalk, variables can be of type: class; class–instance; instance; temporary; global; or pool.

View One of the three types of *class* which are part of the *MVC* architecture. Views are responsible for presenting *model* objects in graphical or textual ways on the screen.

Virtual Image The notional memory space of the Smalltalk *virtual machine*. A file holding this information.

Virtual Machine A program running on a real computer, which simulates the standardised 'virtual' computer on which all Smalltalk programs run.

VisualWorks The name of a commercial implementation of the Smalltalk system from ParcPlace Systems, Inc.

Widget A general term for any button, text–entry field, *view* or other device in a graphical user–interface.

Xerox PARC Xerox Palo Alto Research Center, in California.

Index